OLD SHEET MUSIC

OLD SHEET MUSIC

A PICTORIAL HISTORY

MARIAN KLAMKIN

Photographs by Charles Klamkin

HAWTHORN BOOKS, INC.
PUBLISHERS/NEW YORK

OLD SHEET MUSIC

Library of Congress Catalog Card Number: 74-18695

ISBN: 0–8015–5500–0

1 2 3 4 5 6 7 8 9 10

CONTENTS

ACKNOWLEDGMENTS

Most of the sheet music illustrated in this book came from two major sources. For permission to photograph the collection of the music department at the Free Library of Philadelphia and for his valuable help and advice I am extremely grateful to Mr. Sam M. Dennison. For access and permission to photograph the collection of popular music at the Brown University Library I would like to thank Mr. Stuart C. Sherman.

I am indebted to many others who made their personal collections of old sheet music available to me. Among them are Barbara Fried, Dan Calabrese, Helen C. Collins, and Beatrice Walters Alexander. I am also grateful to Joan Rainer for her valuable research assistance.

OLD SHEET MUSIC

SHEET MUSIC AS AN EXPRESSION OF AMERICAN POPULAR ART

Popular songs have played an important role in America's history, and the subject of our musical heritage has been written about by musicologists for many years. They have made us aware of the wealth of music and lyrics that have been written to express every human emotion and record every momentous event in our history. Representative popular songs of America tell us something about the individual and collective passions we have experienced, the dances we danced, the games we played, the way we spoke, the foods we ate, the clothes we wore, our prejudices, our wars, and our accomplishments. The improvement in our methods of getting from one place to another has been written about by lyricists who treated the subject seriously or with some humor. Our architectural accomplishments have been recorded in song and our national heroes have often been made to seem larger than life by the popular songwriters of our country. The combinations of musical and verbal expression in the vernacular style have been analyzed over and over by historians of this century.

What has been published *between* the covers of popular sheet music is a subject that has been covered rather fully. However, the covers, themselves, are the contemporary artists' interpretation of the popular songs that they were hired to illustrate, and this aspect of popular sheet music has been largely ignored. From an artistic point of view sheet music is unique in that almost from its inception, the published piece of popular music has brought three forms of art together in a manner where they are interdependent for the final success of the product. It is true that if a song isn't one that appeals to a great segment of the population the most attractive and innovative cover in the world won't help it, and some superbly illustrated covers can be found on songs that never made anybody's hit parade. However, there are many collectors to whom the cover art is an important element of the history of

American sheet music. The handsome lithograph on a piece of early nineteenth-century sheet music may have been its only reason for having been saved from destruction. In addition, the early lithographs are as important an expression of American popular art as are the words and notes to be found within the covers of a published song.

If we consider American popular sheet music as being made up of three elements, rather than the two (words and music) that are most often studied and discussed, it should be obvious that the interdependence is important. To the musicologist, written and printed music only comes to life when it is played. To the sheet music collector, it is the ownership of the physical object that is important. What the piece of sheet music looks like, what the subject matter represents, and where the song fits into our artistic as well as our musical history are important points. Songs that represent our political, social, and economic life are in high demand. When the cover artists added their expressive comments to the songwriters' products this becomes important to collectors as well.

There are as many categories in which American sheet music can be collected as there are ways of rhyming "moon" with "June." The sheet music of songs that have enjoyed great popularity at various times in our history has been collected by musicologists for a very long time. Their interest in how words and music have been put together to express popular thought and emotion has led to the preservation of some of our earliest examples of music. But for the most part pieces of sheet music have been discarded once their popularity has run its course. A song that is especially popular over a long period of time becomes what is known in the music business as a "standard," and it might be reprinted many times in a variety of instrumental or vocal arrangements. However, printed sheet music is ephemeral, made to be sold cheaply, and is often thrown out to make room for the next popular tune.

When it comes to popular songs the American public is quite fickle. The song hit that is on everyone's list of favorites this year will be forgotten in a matter of months, and even those songs that are considered standards can remain almost completely unknown by millions who are only interested in the latest popular hits. It is difficult today for anyone over forty to believe that there is an entire generation of Americans who have probably never heard (or if they did, could not identify) that great Mitchell Parish–Hoagy Carmichael hit, "Stardust," written in 1929. While that song enjoyed three decades of popularity, there are few of the generation that heard it who would want to revive "Three Little Fishies" which had a huge popular success in 1939. That was the same year that the movie *The Wizard of Oz* was released, and if the songs from that film are known to another generation it is probably because the medium of television has kept E. Y. Harburg's marvelous lyrics and Harold Arlen's great tunes alive.

As a collecting hobby sheet music has had a rather sketchy career. Some of our earliest sheet music has been preserved simply because the covers were too attractive to be thrown out. This is especially true of nineteenth-century lithographed pictorial covers. Other music was saved for sentimental reasons—Grandmother used to play it on the piano while the family stood around and sang. Since a lot of early sheet music was written and printed to help celebrate great events in our history or to commemorate our heroes, these types of music were put away and preserved by historians.

Although hundreds of thousands of pieces of sheet music were published during the first half of the nineteenth century so little of it has survived that it makes collecting in this period rather difficult and expensive. It is probable that a lot more pieces of this period have been saved than we think and that they will come to light when their owners realize that they are of some value to collectors.

To those collectors who look for the most artistic and illustrative covers certain rare examples of good artwork are coveted, and in many cases only one or two examples of a particular lithograph might still exist. These collectors are interested in the development of printing as a popular art form as well as in words and music. Except for this group of collectors the decorative aspects of American sheet music have been overlooked. Library collections of sheet music from the first half of the nineteenth century are usually part of a university music department and have not been known nor have they been generally available to art historians. Yet they form a most important category of the history of American printing and lithography. The collectors and museums that search for the once popular prints of Currier and Ives often are not aware that some of the earliest and best work done by Currier was as illustrations for sheet music covers.

Every major city of the first half of the nineteenth century had its leading engravers who did a steady business designing and printing song sheets and covers for popular music. The same engravers who printed military badges and broadsides to welcome General Lafayette on his triumphal return to this country in 1824 also published the hastily written musical pieces that were played by the bands that performed at the celebrations.

Although early nineteenth-century song sheets with decorative covers are the cream of any sheet music collection, this is only one aspect of an ever-growing field of collecting. Today's young people approach the hobby from a different point of view. They are interested in the history of the development of the American musical theater and the twentieth-century story of American musical film. A lot of pertinent information concerning this interest is available on the covers of the sheet music published in this century. The composers, lyricists, choreographers, and stars of the shows can easily be documented from the credits and titles found on the handsome Art Nouveau and Art Deco covers that were designed to help sell the hit songs. It is probably secondary, although certainly not unimportant, that these covers from the first half of this century represent fine examples of the popular art and letter styles that developed from before the turn of the century to the period of World War II. In this aspect, the sheet music cover art is not unlike the poster art of the period. In many cases the same design *was* used for the posters that advertised the shows and films.

Illustrated sheet music covers are examples of the development of popular art, photography, and color printing. Usually, although there are a few exceptions, the least expensive method of making a striking and attractive cover for each popular song was used. More often than not early twentieth-century song sheet covers were printed in two colors, and the designers were faced with the challenge of devising an appealing design that could be printed cheaply. The sheet music business in the first half of this century was as important, relatively speaking, as the record industry is today. The major difference between the two industries is that the publisher was not willing to spend large amounts for the design of sheet music covers, since each sheet sold for less than a dollar and the printing and design costs had to be kept as low as possible.

It is obvious that most of the artists who earned a living designing covers for popular songs in this century thought very little of their work. Only a minimal amount of all the sheet music published has signed cover designs. If there is any identification at all it is usually by the art company for whom the artists worked. For the artists it was a job, and they turned out thousands of handsome covers that can never be identified as theirs. The exceptions exist only where an artist was hired especially for a particular design and was known for his illustrations in some other area of commercial art. Signed covers by well-known artists are considered a rarity and are coveted by collectors, especially if the artist later became known for his work in the fine arts. The most important of covers of this type is the "United States Military Academy Song of the Graduates" of 1852. The lithographed cover was designed by "Cadet Whistler."

Early popular songs of a patriotic or political nature such as "Yankee Doodle" or "Free America" were important in our history and are collected today even though the melodies for both were "borrowed" from the British. War songs have had a great influence on our attitude and spirit, and it is little wonder that many collectors specialize in this category. American heroes, from George Washington to Charles Lindbergh, had hundreds of songs written in their honor, and while the music and lyrics have long been forgotten, the pieces of sheet music and the decorative covers of some of them are in strong demand today for their importance in American history. Not only the famous but the infamous had their share of songs written for them. All important national accomplishments have been extolled in popular song. One of the earliest of these was "The Meeting of the Waters on Hudson and Erie" dedicated to DeWitt Clinton at the opening of the Erie Canal in 1825. Songs of pioneering days, the old West, developments in transportation, and regional songs are all of great interest today.

There were few facets of American life that were not recorded in popular song and by the artists on the covers. We celebrated national disasters in song as often as we did national accomplishments. The songwriters expressed our emotions for us, and the artists interpreted those emotions on the covers of the songs.

It would be impossible to collect sheet music of America's past without learning a lot about the country's history and certainly a great deal about the development of popular art styles. If we think our current wave of nostalgia is unique we have only to turn back the sheet music pages to see that early in this century songwriters were already writing nostalgically about the "gay nineties."

Many specialist-collectors in fields seemingly far removed from music have long collected the songs that relate to their particular hobbies. Automobile historians and collectors of car memorabilia search for copies of "The Automobile Honeymoon" (1902), on the front cover of which is a couple in a speeding car and a picture of Lew Dockstader, a singer who made the song popular in its time. Two other songs, "Get an Automobile" (1906) and "Git a Horse" (1902), might be of little interest to musicologists but are very desirable items for car buffs. The more popular standards such as "He'd Have to Get Under—Get Out and Get Under" (1913) and "In My Merry Oldsmobile" (1905) are probably more available, but auto collectors also search for rarities and would rather find copies of "My Automobile Girl from New Orleans" (1900) or "The Little Ford Rambled Right Along," published in 1914.

Some of our popular songs have grown in importance as time has passed and given them new historical meaning. There is a new interest in songs related to early aspects of the women's movement, for instance, and the irony of the songwriter's humor in poking fun at the petroleum czars of the nineteenth century is beginning to strike us as often as those newly made millionaires struck a lucrative well in 1865.

No book on American popular music would be complete without a discussion of the development of the phonograph and the radio. Both of these important inventions helped spread popular songs across the land in this century and led to the growth of New York as the music center of America. They also ultimately led to the demise of the music publishing industry. Big bands, great performers, musical theater, and film are all part of the American pop scene of this century. The story of how popular music went from rag to jazz to swing and ultimately to rock is also illustrated in sheet music covers.

The subject matter covered through two hundred years of American popular songwriting is so wide and varied that it would be impossible to cover everything in one book. What will be emphasized here are the *most* popular of popular songs of America—the "Oldies but Goodies" that we all recognize. Also, there will be some discussion of the categories in which many collectors have been specializing for years. When we concern ourselves with the music of this century, especially all those songs written during the heyday of Tin Pan Alley, it becomes clear that many of the old songs were printed and sold in huge quantities. This doesn't mean that many of the most popular songs from that era still exist in comparable quantity. The sheet music publishing business only exists today as a very minor part of the recording industry, and it is extremely difficult to purchase new sheet music for popular tunes. Paper items are not generally kept, and the old songs were thrown out through the years. This makes collecting sheet music from this century somewhat difficult, but it is a challenge that all collectors enjoy.

Emphasis in the following chapters will be on the development of printed popular music in America, the performers who popularized the music, and most especially, the visual aspects of sheet music. Previously, a lot of attention has been given to the nineteenth-century lithographed sheet music of America. True, the covers are handsome and have now been elevated to the category of fine graphic art. Sheet music of this century has been largely ignored. The great popular songs of the turn of the century, the show tunes, and the musical movie songs have been studied from every aspect but the printed sheets on which they appear. This is an area in which today's collector needs some guidance, and this aspect of the music publishing industry will be emphasized.

Out of the roughly two and a half million popular songs that have been written and published in this country, obviously the number that can be discussed and illustrated here is limited, but the illustrations are representative of the many types of sheet music that have been published. We will look at published American sheet music from its visual aspects and from the collector's point of view, with the audio turned down.

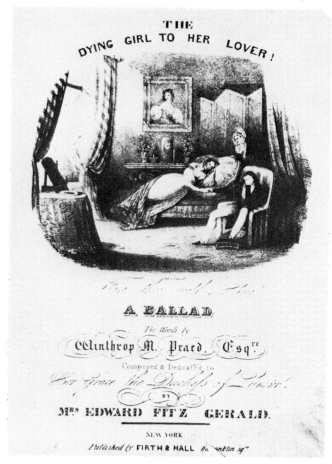

The staple of American popular music has always been the ballad. Endicott lithograph, New York, ca. 1835.

Sheet music cover with illustration of American band. Tailor & Smith lithograph, Philadelphia, ca. 1850.

Comic songs were popular through the nineteenth century. "Corn Cobs" published by Endicott, New York, 1836.

Music was published locally throughout the nineteenth century. This is first song published in California.

EARLY PUBLISHERS
AND LITHOGRAPHERS

There are some problems that beset the collector in dating late eighteenth-century and early nineteenth-century American sheet music. The word "music" was not mentioned specifically in the Federal Copyright Act until 1831. Prior to that time some music was copyrighted as "books." In addition the copyright deposits of sheet music on file in the Library of Congress are far from complete. Until 1870 the places designated as depositories changed from time to time and much was lost in transition. For instance in 1790 the secretary of state received all first copies, and in 1831 the U.S. District Court received all first copies. By 1831 it was designated that the copies collected by the court be transmitted once a year to the secretary of state. It was not until 1870 that all recorded copyright material was sent directly to the Library of Congress. Although that institution now is the repository of close to two and a half million pieces of sheet music, the collection is still not complete. In addition many early songs were undated and unrecorded and it is probable that much of it has been lost to us forever.

Some of the existing undated sheet music can be dated in a variety of ways. Knowledge of the publishers and lithographers and when they worked can be a helpful tool. Often the songs whose subject matter deals with an aspect of history can be dated through a knowledge of when the event occurred. The early publishers did not usually depend upon the publication of sheet music as their only means of livelihood and sometimes combined this endeavor with other seemingly unrelated occupations such as barber, tavern keeper, or even umbrella maker. In some cases the engraver of the cover picture used a picture of the store where the music was sold as part of the cover design. Sometimes a publisher's imprint is helpful in dating an early piece of music.

Many of our early songs were not published as complete music sheets at all. The words were printed on a broadside or in a periodical and were sung to an already popular tune. This is particularly true of songs written for special occasions when a lot of copies would be needed, such as on the occasion of Lafayette's visit in 1824–25. The cost of printing a poem on a small slip of paper was considerably less than printing an entire music sheet. For such occasions a local poet was often chosen for the honor of composing verses to fit familiar music.

One way of making a new song available to the general public was to have the verses printed in local newspapers. One of our earliest patriotic songs, "The Liberty Song," was written in 1768 by John Dickinson, and it first appeared in the *Boston Gazette,* and "Liberty's Call," written either by Francis Hopkinson or John Mason, was published first in the *Pennsylvania Packet.* An early child's song, "The Alphabet," was printed first as a broadside and then was reprinted in the *Constitutional Gazette.*

It wasn't until late in the eighteenth century or early in the nineteenth century that American popular songs began to be illustrated with lithographed covers. Lithography, or stone drawing, was invented in the latter part of the eighteenth century in Bavaria by Alois Senefelder. Its principle was the fact that grease and water will not mix. The method of printing from stone spread rapidly, and by the early part of the nineteenth century there were many American lithographers at work, and not a few of them derived at least part of their livelihood in the making of sheet music for popular distribution.

The method used in preparing a stone for printing was first to cut the stone to the right size, which would be slightly larger than the overall size of the print to be made. The stone was several inches thick, and both sides had to be absolutely level and the front and back perfectly parallel. The surface on which the drawing was to be made was then ground with fine sand or glass placed between the lithograph stone and a slightly larger stone. The abrasion left a smooth surface on which the artist could work.

The artist made a drawing in reverse on the stone's surface with a greasy crayon, and when the drawing was complete the stone was given a bath of gum arabic and nitric acid. This solution attacked only that part of the stone's surface that was untouched by the crayon and left the drawing itself in slight relief.

The stone was then thoroughly washed to stop the action of the acid and was then ready for printing. It was put in the press, wetted thoroughly, and spread by roller with a special lithographic ink. Since the drawing was raised, the ink only adhered to the design and not the background, which had been eaten away by the acid bath. A sheet of paper was then placed on the stone and pressure applied. When the print was pulled from the press it was ready for sale.

Of all early nineteenth-century lithographed sheet music covers those most coveted by collectors are the ones that have been hand-colored. When this was to be done the first copies from the press were sent to a professional colorist, who was usually a local artist, who colored the print in flat shades of watercolor. He derived his shadows from the lithograph. Upon the approval of the colorist's embellishments the master copy would then be given to a group of women and girls who simply followed the master copy. The technique was similar to a child filling in the lines in his coloring book. The lithographed sheet music was often offered to the public either colored or uncolored with the extra charge for color being as little as five cents.

Among the first commercial printers to see the possible applications for the new art of lithography to the publishing of sheet music were William and John Pendleton of Boston. An apprentice of theirs, Nathaniel Currier, was fifteen years old when he came to work for them, and he remained with the firm for five years. Following his apprenticeship, Currier worked for a year for M. E. D. Brown of Philadelphia and then went to New York where he formed a partnership with a man named William Stodart, who owned a music store at 167 Broadway from 1831 to 1834. Since Currier was already familiar with the design of sheet music through his experience with the Pendletons, it is probable that he thought the same type of business in New York would be lucrative enough to support him. Fortunately, he was ambitious enough to team up later on in his career with another partner, and the printmakers became known throughout the country, not for their sheet music covers but for their inexpensive lithographed genre pictures that by midcentury decorated almost every home in the country.

Most of the existing examples of Currier sheet music covers date between the years 1835 to 1839 when Currier was in business by himself. He did work for several publishers, among whom were J. Disturnell and J. H. Bufford. His work was also in demand by publishers outside of New York City. Nathaniel Currier was not the only lithographer who designed sheet music covers in his time, but he is by far the best known, although there are many print collectors who know little of his sheet music work. Music collectors are fully aware of the importance of the work young Currier did in the cover design field, and Currier prints are perhaps the most precious owned by any collectors who specialize in early signed lithographed sheet music.

By 1870 there were hundreds of lithographers in all of the larger cities in the country who, along with other assignments, were engaged in the printing of sheet music. In New York City alone almost a hundred lithographers can be listed in 1870. Many of these lithographers had one or more artists working for them. Collectors search for examples of the work of the better known and most prolific lithographers. However, it should be remembered that all pictorial lithographed sheet music covers of the first half of the nineteenth century have some value, either artistic, historical, or both.

Among the best-known and most prolific nineteenth-century sheet music lithographers are Bouvé, Sharp, Bufford, Pendleton, and Prang of Boston; Endicott and Swett, John Penniman and Edward Weber of Baltimore; Blake and Willis, Currier, Bofford Brothers, Thayer, Endicott, Fleetwood, Sarony, and Lewis and Brown of New York; P. S. Duval, Sinclair, Childs, and Inman of Philadelphia. As the technique of lithography spread, lithographers went into business in St. Louis, San Francisco, Chicago, Washington, D.C., and many other cities across the country.

If the lithographers of the first half of the nineteenth century form a confusing story it is because they went in and out of business with some frequency, joined in partnership with others, migrated from city to city, and employed extra help when business warranted it. It is known that the earliest music publisher started in business in the United States in 1768 and that by the end of the century there was at least one major publisher in each city then settled. By the middle of the next century the music publishing industry was widespread, and songs were being published at a great rate from coast to coast.

As the music publishing business progressed in the nineteenth century printing processes were developed that were cheaper and easier to use than hand lithography. Toward the end of the century photography replaced hand designs, and often a combination of artist-designed covers with photography was used. While the lithographer signed his picture in the plate, the artists who designed the later covers remained anonymous. It is seldom that after the 1860s we find even initials to identify the designer of a sheet music cover.

For those collectors involved only with music of this century interest lies in innovative cover design and photographic records of the performers who introduced the songs. Imaginative layouts and decorative drawings that show remarkable talent as manifested in a form of popular art can be found in abundance in music covers of this century. The careers of our best-known stars of stage and screen can be traced on a collection of sheet music covers.

Towards the end of the nineteenth century there were few song sheets published where color or particularly good art work were used. Most covers were black and white printing. This kept costs down and the music sold anyway so there was little incentive for the publishers to seek out imaginative artists. There was one man who was largely responsible for designing handsome color covers after the turn of the century. It is probable that his name, like many others that have never been recorded because the design of sheet music covers was not thought to be of any artistic importance, might have been forgotten had he not gone on to become a lyricist and librettist in his later years.

Gene Buck was born in Detroit in 1885. He had some art training at the Detroit Art Academy and then found a job as a designer for a Detroit stationer and printer who produced all the sheet music covers for Whitney and Warner, an important publisher in Tin Pan Alley. Buck designed posterlike color covers which soon became the rage in the music publishing world and started a trend back to decorative sheet music. Remick, another publishing firm, bought out Whitney and Warner, and Buck was hired to design all of the song covers the company published. He created over five thousand cover designs until he developed a case of blindness and had to stop working for eight months. Fortunately, the blindness was temporary and when he recovered his sight he moved to New York where he arrived practically penniless.

By this time, Buck was well-known in Tin Pan Alley and he was able to get a new job designing sheet music covers for other companies. In 1911 he wrote his first lyric for the song, "Daddy Has a Sweetheart and Mother Is Her Name," with music by David Stamper. The song was included in the 1912 edition of Florenz Ziegfeld's *Follies,* and in the following year Buck and Stamper had three numbers in the *Follies.* Buck provided lyrics for many of Ziegfeld's shows in the next seventeen years. Among his hits were "Hello, Frisco, Hello," "Tulip Time," and " 'Neath the South Sea Moon." His close relationship to Ziegfeld led to Buck's discovery of many performers who went on to become stars. Among them were Ed Wynn, Will Rogers, and Eddie Cantor. Between 1927 and 1931 Buck became a producer, and in 1931 he worked for Ziegfeld in the last *Follies* produced by Ziegfeld himself. Buck died in Manhasset, Long Island, in 1957, after spending his final years in doing executive work for ASCAP. A collector could easily specialize in sheet music covers designed by Gene Buck and in the music for which Buck wrote lyrics in his New York years. Remembered more for his lyrics than his art, Gene Buck was largely responsible for the many attractive and colorful covers to have been printed in the early years of this century.

If anyone doubts that a large part of sheet music collecting is involved with the development of printing in America he has only to compare the painstaking process of the early artists in lithography like Nathaniel Currier to the running off of thousands of copies of decorative sheet music in the thirties, forties, and fifties. Modern presses made the publication of music a simple process. We may easily argue that the lithographed covers, printed on good quality paper, were far more attractive and enduring than the sheet music of this century and that the earlier element of handwork cannot be disallowed. However, it is also necessary to consider that a musician could buy a piece of popular sheet music in the early nineteenth century for twenty-five or thirty cents. A piece of contemporary sheet music, when one can find it today, can still be purchased for less than a dollar, and top price for a single song is one dollar fifty. The music publishing industry, currently beset with many problems, is almost alone in keeping its product available to the masses at a relatively low price.

Each period in our history has produced its own form of popular art, and it is of interest that the art that has been produced to represent America's popular music of the past two centuries is the only form of popular art that has been available as a bonus or gift from the music publishers. All the covers were ever intended to do was to help sell the song. Music covers have been our earliest and most consistent form of decorative packaging.

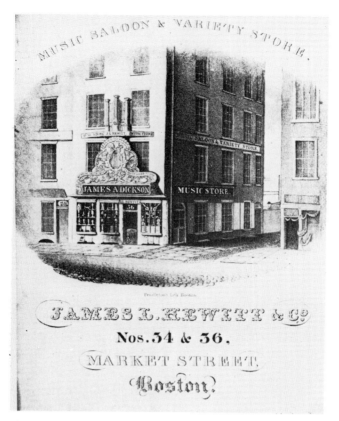

Sheet music was published by music and variety stores, and often publishers put picture of their building on cover. Boston, ca. 1830.

Cover with lithograph by J. H. Bufford, New York, 1830.

Polka written for "Our American Cousin," Endicott lithograph, New York, 1859.

"All Around My Hat," comic song with cover lithographed by Endicott, New York, ca. 1840.

Cover lithographed by A. Hoen & Co., Baltimore, ca. 1850.

Cover lithographed by Thayer, Boston, 1844.

Lithograph by Nathaniel Currier, New York, 1847.

By end of nineteenth century lithographed covers were no longer being made, and most sheet music had black and white printed covers. Song first published 1897, but this cover design is from 1905 edition.

PATRIOTIC
AND POLITICAL MUSIC

A good patriotic air will stir the blood of any American, and the songs of this type that have become classics are a collecting category in themselves. Long studies have been done on the origins of such well-known songs as "Yankee Doodle," "America" (which every school child starts out believing is "My country! *Tears* of thee"), and our national anthem, "The Star-Spangled Banner."

Early editions of "Dixie," "Hail Columbia," "Columbia, the Gem of the Ocean," and other music of a patriotic nature are in demand and constitute a specialty in sheet music collecting. "Yankee Doodle" is the most popular and perhaps the oldest of all American patriotic songs and is easily recognized throughout the world. The tune is not of American origin and the earliest printed record of it is in *Selection of Scotch, English, Irish, and Foreign Aires for the Fife, Violin, or German Flute*, which was published in Glasgow in 1782. The catchy tune was sung or played in various ballad operas abroad, but there is also a theory, perhaps just wishful thinking on the part of the patriotic theorists, that it originated in the colonies and then went across the ocean only to return again where the earliest printed record of it is in the "Federal Overture" published by Benjamin Carr in 1794.

Whatever the origins of the tune, it is known that the British troops used it to poke fun at the Yankees and that the Americans then turned the tune to taunt British troops even before the Revolution. There is only one known copy of the "Federal Overture" but there are other slightly later versions of the song which are in public and private collections.

The background of the origins of our national anthem has also been told often, but since a copy of the first edition would be considered the most important single item in any patriotic sheet music collection, it bears repeating here. The "Star-Spangled Banner" was written in 1814, during the war with Britain. Francis Scott Key was aboard a boat where he had been sent to arrange for the release of a prisoner who was a friend of his. The boat was moored off the port of Baltimore and while Key was still aboard, the boat was sent orders to bomb Fort McHenry. The sight of Old Glory flying above the fort while the bombardment was carried out inspired Key to pull out an envelope and write down the lines that start, "Oh say can you see. . . ."

The tune to which the words were set, "To Anacreon in Heaven," was well known in America at the time. It was the official song of the Anacreontic Society of London, a social, quasi-Masonic group. The composer was a British musician, John Stafford Smith, who had had other popular successes and was a well-known composer and musician. Both tune and lyrics have undergone some changes over the years which came about through popular use and not through an official decision. The song was America's unofficial anthem for many years, and during the Civil War new martial lyrics were written for it. In 1889 the secretary of the navy ordered that the song be played at all naval installations during the flag-raising and -lowering ceremonies, and in 1903 the army began using it for special ceremonies. By 1913 a movement was launched to have the song accepted as a national anthem but Congress failed to act. The Veterans of Foreign Wars began pushing for the song's national adoption in 1928, and finally in 1931 Public Law 823 was passed, making the song America's official and only national anthem.

There are many songs well-known to us today that were written during the Civil War period and some collectors specialize further in songs of the Confederacy, which are somewhat more difficult to find than the more widely distributed Union songs. Confederate collectors look for early copies of "The War Song of Dixie" (Dixie), "Dixie Doodle," "The Drummer Boy of Shiloh," "For Bales!" "God Save the South," "Maryland! My Maryland!" "Our First President's Quickstep," and many other rebel songs.

Union songs of the Civil War period are more familiar. One of the most famous is "When Johnny Comes Marching Home," but there is also "Marching Through Georgia," "The Sour Apple Tree," "Tramp! Tramp! Tramp!" "Tenting on the Old Camp Ground," "The Drummer Boy of Shiloh," and the rousing "Battle Cry of Freedom." There is also sheet music written about the scrip used during the war, two of which are the "Shin-Plaster Jig" and "How Are You Green-Backs!"

No American war was without its music until later in this century when the nation became involved in two wars about which the songwriters could find little to say. There are collectors' items from the Spanish-American war, and hundreds of songs were written that became popular during both World Wars. World War I songs are especially popular with collectors today.

When the patriotism of an entire nation must be worked up to fever pitch to increase production, sacrifice lives, and create an atmosphere where hardship will not be resented, the songwriters come forth with contributions that have an enormous effect on the nation. The country's leading performers promote the patriotism through popular songs, and one can almost say that the best thing to come out of the World Wars was the American popular music written during those conflicts.

If we look at the songs that were written during World Wars I and II we can understand the important part music plays in our national life and the necessity for humor in our most serious moments. In 1918 Irving Berlin wrote "Oh! How I Hate to Get up in the Morning," and the following year Sam M. Lewis and Joe Young wrote the song popularized by Sopie Tucker, "How Ya Gonna Keep 'em Down on the Farm? (After They've Seen Paree)." "Lafayette—We Hear You Calling" was in a more serious vein, but another song of the War was "When Alexander Takes His Ragtime Band to France," and some soldiers sang "Would You Rather Be a Colonel with an Eagle on Your Shoulder, or a Private with a Chicken on Your Knee?" A few of the sentimental tunes were "Till We Meet Again," "When You Come Back," and "Three Wonderful Letters From Home." One of America's greatest war songs was written in 1917. "Over There" by George M. Cohan is the one song with which World War I is most identified.

Irving Berlin came through for his country again in World War II with his hit show, *This is the Army,* and the length of the war is represented in the huge amount of both great and terrible songs from the forties that had to do with some aspect of the struggle. In addition to the sentimental, humorous, and patriotic songs there were many that were written expressly for propaganda purposes. Americans were told through a rousing song to "Buy a Bond Today" or "A Slip of the Lip Could Sink a Ship." During the early part of the draft a popular song was "Goodbye Dear, I'll Be Back in a Year." Jimmy Dorsey's Orchestra popularized the flying song "Comin' in on a Wing and a Prayer," and the leading songwriters did their part by writing war songs such as "Vict'ry Polka" (words by Samuel Cahn and music by Johnny Mercer), "G.I. Jive" (words and music by Johnny Mercer), and "Praise the Lord and Pass the Ammunition" (words and music by Frank Loesser). Loesser also wrote "What Do You Do in the Infantry?" a song to which the army marched during World War II.

Most war songs are forgotten within a few months of their publication. A few become all-time hits. Perhaps the best-remembered song of World War II is "God Bless America" by Irving Berlin. All war songs are collected today. Although the most popular were published in huge amounts, few of them survive in good condition.

Patriotic or political events were also recorded in popular music. An early event that had its own music written for it was the visit of General Lafayette to America in 1824–25. Lafayette visited every city and large town in the country during his sentimental journey to America as the last living Revolutionary War general, and a lot of music, mostly in the form of marches and quick-steps, was written and played during parades and balls. One of the few "Welcome Lafayette" pieces that had words was written by William Strickland and is illustrated with an engraving of the triumphal arch Strickland designed for Lafayette's visit to Philadelphia. The song, "Come Honor the Brave!" was set to the tune of "My Heart's in the Highlands."

An extremely rare piece of sheet music that is important, not only for its

Lafayette associations, but because it is the earliest piece of sheet music that shows an American stage performer, Mr. Roberts, in blackface is "Massa Georgee Washington and General La Fayette." The song was performed at Theatre Chatham Gardens in New York in 1824 and is the forerunner of thousands of black dialect songs that would be performed throughout the nineteenth century.

If American songwriters have been generous with their talent in writing music to rouse patriotic fervor during wartime and patriotic events, they also have been prolific in supplying music during political campaigns. Songwriters, either from their own inspiration or because they were paid to do it, have written songs for every American political candidate.

Musical pieces and songs have been written for both the losing and winning candidates of every American presidential election. The songs vary in quality and purpose as much as do the men for whom they were written, but much of the music from the earlier elections was written to be performed at inaugural ceremonies. Many other "president" songs were used as campaign aids, since everyone knows that there's nothing like a catchy tune to convince the country of a man's fitness for office.

Many of the presidential pieces were suitably illustrated according to the popular art style of the times. A study of the political song covers can give the collector some idea of the changes in styles of cover art as well as changes in the style of popular songwriting over the years. The earliest pieces of popular music had only elaborately engraved titles to decorate them. When there is a picture as well, as in the case of "Grand National March," written for President Andrew Jackson, it is a bonus for the collector. Two Harrison pieces have handsome lithographs on the covers: one a battle scene by Sharp and the other the president in uniform on his horse by Sinclair.

Some presidents seem to have been more favored as subjects of music than others. Usually, this had nothing to do with the popularity of the man, but the length of time in office or the available finances during the campaigns. The well-financed campaign of William McKinley was probably responsible for the many songs written for him. There were a great many songs written for Franklin Delano Roosevelt. He was president for a long time and the wartime patriotism of America's songwriters led to the many F. D. R. songs that were written for campaigns and inaugurals and in between these events as well.

If the songwriters and music publishers were generous in honoring presidents during their terms in office, they were even more prolific following the untimely death of a president. The greater amount of the many Lincoln songs that exist were written after Lincoln's assassination. In 1881 the Wm. A. Pond Company of New York lost no time in publishing "President Garfield's Funeral March" on the cover of which is a portrait of the president suitably surrounded with every mourning symbol the artist could think of.

In the nineteenth century mourning was a favorite indoor sport, and one of the saddest Lincoln memorial songs is "Little Tad," written after the president's death. A quote on the cover explains: " 'TAD' the pet name of President Lincoln's youngest son—he was a great favorite with his father, as may be inferred from the fact that Mrs. Lincoln while at the bedside of her dying husband, exclaimed, 'Oh! Bring our TAD here! For he loves TAD so well that I know he will speak to him!' " Nineteenth-century songwriters and the people who bought their products doted on disaster.

Presidential songs were not always written to honor a president. The song, "Andy Veto," was written to point out one of the charges brought against Andrew Johnson during his impeachment proceedings. The charge of Johnson's corrupt use of power earned the president the nickname that became the title of a song of political commentary.

Another interesting political cover is "Roll Along, Roll Along, Shout the Campaign Battle Song," which was written for the Hayes campaign. The political cartoon shows Uncle Sam riding atop the Hayes wagon which is being pulled toward the White House by oxen that represent the states. Around the White House is written, "Honest Money Paid Here."

The more colorful the presidential candidate, the more he inspired composers, lyricists, and cover artists. Theodore Roosevelt provided inspiration for many songs before, during, and even after his term in office. His military life was recorded, and his avocation as a big-game hunter became the subject of musical pieces.

Some campaign songs were adapted from popular music. For instance, Truman's song was "I'm Just Wild About Harry," and it was originally written in 1921 for an all-black revue called *Shuffle Along*. "They Like Ike" was written by Irving Berlin in praise of Eisenhower before he became president and was introduced in the musical *Call Me Madam* in 1950. Later on, it was adapted as a most appropriate campaign song.

If writing songs for a political candidate were insurance that he would be voted president there would have been no losers in our political history. If there are not quite as many songs surviving for the candidates for the presidency who did not make it to the White House, it is not because they weren't written but because not many of them were saved. The earliest presidential "loser" songs that we find today were written for Henry Clay, "the Great Compromiser." The first time Clay ran for president was in the election of 1824 when he finished fourth. In 1832 he was defeated by Andrew Jackson and in 1844, when he tried again, he was narrowly defeated for the high office by James K. Polk. William Jennings Bryan ties with Henry Clay for being a candidate three times and losing every election. "Bryan and Free Silver March" represents his first nomination in 1896 as leader of the Democratic party. "Turning Point March" was written for Bryan's second attempt in 1900, and it wasn't a turning point at all when Bryan was defeated by McKinley. "Line Up for Bryan" was no help to the experienced candidate who again lost the election, this time to William Howard Taft, in 1908.

If the country never had the opportunity to experience "Better Times with Al" (Smith) it was not the fault of the songwriters. We didn't find out what might have happened under the leadership of "Our Landon," nobody did

"Win with Wilkie" (*or* Wallace), and those who thought we could "Do It with Dewey" didn't. The Republicans who sang "Go with Goldwater" didn't go very far at all.

Patriotic and political songs are a part of America's musical heritage and are collected by specialists in that field. There are hundreds of songs and musical pieces that fit into this category and together they form a musical and political history of the country. Although much of the music and lyrics are less than memorable a representative collection becomes interesting political commentary on the men who have attempted to gain America's highest office.

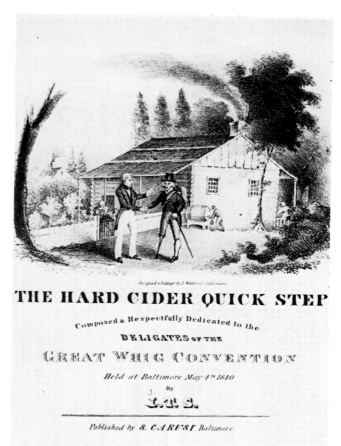

Sheet music written and published for visit of General Lafayette to United States in 1824. Song and engraving by William Strickland, Philadelphia.

"The Hard Cider Quick Step," E. Weber & Co. lithograph, 1840.

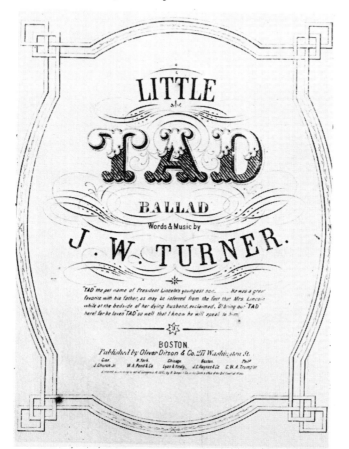

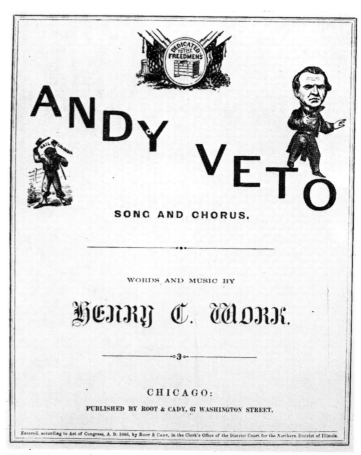

Sad ballad written after Lincoln was shot. Published by Oliver Ditson in 1865.

Political song written during Andrew Johnson's impeachment proceedings in 1866.

Political cartoon adorns Hayes campaign song cover of 1875.

Descriptive cover of "Guiteau's March to Hades" shows assassin of President Garfield as Devil, 1881.

Music written to memory of Ulysses S. Grant shows wreaths with all of the states written on them surrounding cross with Grant's name on it, 1885.

Music written in honor of President Cleveland's marriage to his young ward was popular in its day, 1886.

One of many songs written for Theodore Roosevelt. This one was written when he was on safari after he had finished being president, 1909.

William Howard Taft campaign song, 1908.

Many songs were written for F.D.R. This one was performed by Dick Powell in a propaganda short subject for National Reconstruction Administration.

Old hit of all-black show, "Shuffle Along" (1921), was used as campaign song for Truman in 1948.

Civil War Union music. Kurz and Seifert lithograph, 1861.

"Greenbacks" has cover showing Civil War scrip. Song was popular minstrel number in 1863. Sarony, Major, and Knapp lithograph.

Song of Civil War Reconstruction period. W. F. Shaw, Philadelphia, publisher. 1874.

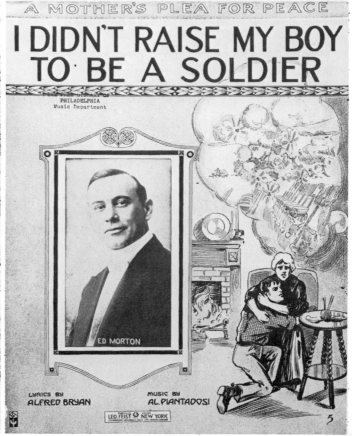

World War I isolationist song, 1915.

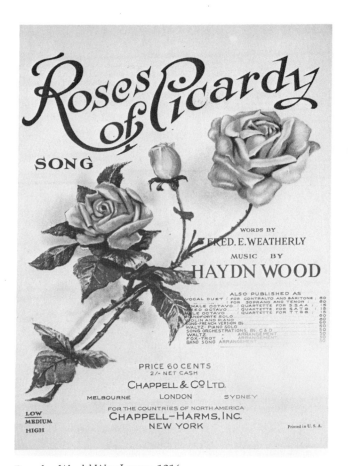

Popular World War I song, 1916.

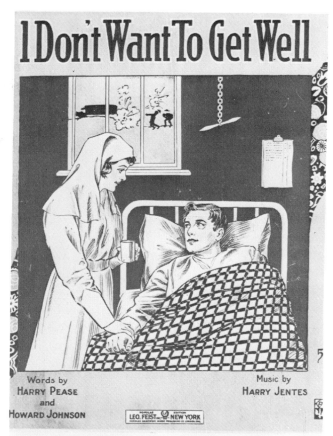

World War I song about a soldier who is in love with a beautiful nurse, 1917.

World War I song was not much of a hit in 1918, but cover of doughboy with camera is original.

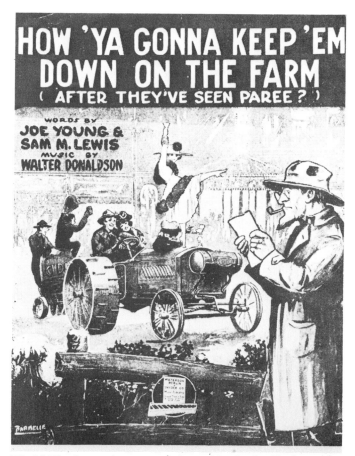

World War I comedy song popularized by Sophie Tucker and Eddie Cantor in 1919.

I'm Getting Tired So I Can Sleep

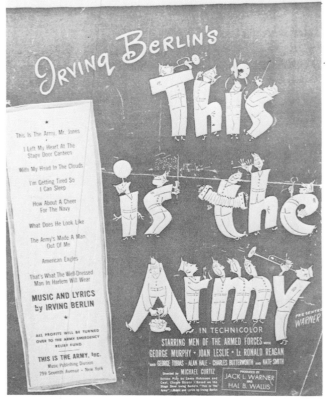

Song from all-soldier review assembled during World War II by Irving Berlin with his own book, music, and lyrics.

First hit song for which Frank Loesser wrote both lyrics and music. It sold over two million records and a million copies of sheet music in 1942. Lyrics were written shortly after Pearl Harbor attack.

Song by Frank Loesser was written in 1943 while he was in service. Introduced by Bing Crosby, it has become infantry's theme song.

Popular World War II song was introduced by Eddie Cantor at an air force base and sold over a million copies.

Songwriters Samuel Cahn and Jule Styne wrote this song in 1943 for war effort.

Songwriter Johnny Mercer's musical contribution to World War II.

Propaganda song, probably unfamiliar to anyone who was not alive during World War II, was played and sung with great frequency after its publication in 1944.

TRANSPORTATION, SPORTS, AND RECREATION

Judging from the amount of songs written in honor of the developments of transportation in nineteenth-century America it is obvious that anything that can move people on land, sea, or in the air is inspiration for the lyricist and composer. We have songs to ships, balloons, dirigibles, trains, trolleys, bicycles, and the greatest American love songs of all—written to the automobile. Of all these the songs extolling or poking fun at the various contraptions devised for air or road travel are in high demand by today's collector.

The earliest transportation songs and musical pieces we can find today are the balloon items. The first successful balloon was built by Joseph and Jacques Montgolfier, sons of a French paper maker, in 1783. The first manned balloon flight was made in Paris by Jean Pilatre de Rozier in October 1783, and a balloon steered by hand-cranked propellers was invented the following year. It had a speed of three miles an hour. The first balloon ascension in the United States took place in 1793, and Francois Blanchard, a Frenchman, was its passenger. These and subsequent balloon ascensions stirred the songwriters' imaginations and inspired handsome sheet music covers. One fascinating cover, for "Le Voyage Aerien," which dates from the second decade of the nineteenth century, is a Duval lithograph after a drawing by Peter Kramer. Instead of the usual basket under the balloon there is a horse and rider. Another colorful cover with a balloon illustration was published in England, but was undoubtedly sold in the United States at the beginning of the nineteenth century. The cover is brilliantly colored in red, green, and blue.

Man had long dreamed of flying like a bird, and various attempts were made in the early 1800s to accomplish this. Orville and Wilbur Wright were finally successful in getting their first controlled, powered machine that was heavier than air off the ground in 1903, and this event and subsequent successes in airborne machinery gave the composers and lyricists another popular subject about which they could write.

In 1911 Glenn Hammond Curtis won a $10,000 prize given by the New York newspaper, the *World*, for the first continuous airplane flight from Albany to New York. Curtis traveled 137 miles in two hours, thirty-two minutes. Shortly afterwards he accomplished a successful airplane landing on water at Mammondsport, New York. It was a great year for airplane records, and later that year Ralph Johnston flew a distance of 101 miles in three hours, fourteen minutes. The ensuing publicity for the acts of daring was undoubtedly the reason for the continued success of the song, "Come Josephine in My Flying Machine (Up She Goes!)," which had been published the previous year. Other airplane songs were to follow.

In 1919 Raymond B. Orteig, owner of a New York hotel, offered a prize of $25,000 to an aviator who could make a nonstop solo flight between New York and Paris. By 1926 Charles A. Lindbergh, financed by a group of St. Louis citizens, decided to try for the prize, and he bought and outfitted a monoplane which he named the *Spirit of St. Louis.* In flying the plane from San Diego, California, where it was built, to New York in twenty-one hours and twenty minutes Lindbergh established a new coast-to-coast record. He left Roosevelt Field, New York, on May 20, 1927, and landed at Le Bourget Field, Paris, thirty-three hours and thirty minutes later. The rest is history, of course, and Lindbergh became America's folk hero. At least a hundred songs were written in honor of Charles Lindbergh, including "Charlie Boy (We Love You)," "Lindbergh the Eagle of the U.S.A.," and "Lucky Lindy." However, the song that is most often associated with the flight and its hero was written in 1924 by Gus Kahn and Ted Fiorito. Since it suited the man and the occasion so aptly, "Charlie My Boy" was played at all celebrations following Lindbergh's triumphal return to the United States.

There were hundreds of songs written for ships and boats and all related subjects. The most desirable ship items for collectors are the illustrated covers with pictures of early sailing ships. Many of these were beautifully hand-colored. Sea chanties are an early form of popular folk music and many of them concerned disasters at sea, a subject which is never out of a sailor's mind. Any song sheets that illustrate the American clipper ships of the latter half of the nineteenth century are of interest today. Songs that represent the development of the steam-propelled ships are also highly collectible, and of special interest to collectors of river memorabilia are the American sidewheeler illustrations on song sheet covers. The cover of "The Lost Steamer" is by Sarony and commemorates the wreck of the *Pacific* in 1856. "The Light House" is of literary interest as well as marine interest since its lyrics were written by Thomas Moore. The lithographed cover is by Duval. An early San Francisco item is "I Do Not Want to Be Drowned," which is dedicated to the survivors of the *Golden-Gate,* which burned at sea.

Other well-remembered shipwrecks are commemorated in song. "He's on a Boat That Sailed Last Wednesday" is a 1913 commemoration of the ill-fated *Mauretania*. "Just as the Boat Went Down" is the first *Titanic* song, and the cover shows an artist's rendition of the ship before and after the disaster. "The Wreck of the *Titanic*" is another disaster item of interest to collectors.

It should come as no surprise that old automobile songs are extremely desirable collectors' items today. There are two standards illustrated in this chapter: "He'd Have to Get Under—Get Out and Get Under (To Fix Up His Automobile)," published in 1913; and "In My Merry Oldsmobile," published in 1905. There are a great many other automobile items, however, many of them handsomely illustrated. One interesting collectible is "I'm Getting Ready For My Mother-in-law," 1906, which has a picture of the mother-in-law being driven over a precipice by her son-in-law.

"The Little Ford Rambled Right Along," published in 1914, has an illustration of a road full of foundered cars except for the "Little Ford" which seems to have no trouble whatsoever. A 1905 item with the euphonious title, "Otto, You Ought to Take Me in Your Auto" is very desirable, as is "On The Old Back Seat of the Henry Ford" published in 1916.

In short, any transportation songs with illustrated covers are in demand today. Trolleys, buses, and especially railroad trains, bridges, and stations are sought and collected by special interest collectors. One especially noteworthy item is "The Rail-Road," published in 1828. This is an early item of railroadiana and the cover illustrates the "Ohio Velocipede" leaving for Wheeling and Cincinnati. Balloons over the man and woman who are waving the passengers good-by have the characters saying, "Don't forget to drop my letter in the Post Office in Wheeling so it may get to New Orleans the next day," and "Give my love to all my nine cousins and tell Aunt Polly that I'll drink tea with her in Cincinnati tomorrow evening and bring the new bonnet and the gigot pattern and the Flounces and All." The artist who illustrated the cover of what is possibly the earliest of all American railroad songs was J. Sands, and the music was published by John Cole of Baltimore.

More easily found today are later railroad songs such as the "Fast Line Gallop" published by Lee and Walker in 1853 or "The Iron Horse" published by the same firm in Philadelphia in 1870. The "North Western Railway Polka," dedicated to the officers of the Chicago North Western Railway and the excursionists of October 12, 1859, is another desirable railroad item. The decorated title page has pictures of the excursion train, a ballroom scene, and uniformed soldiers. An especially good item of railroadiana is "The Limited Express March" published in 1894 but with a cover picture of a steam passenger train and the caption, "The first Railroad Train in America, A.D. 1827."

Bicycling has once again become a fashionable way to exercise and is being touted by the medical profession as a healthy way to strengthen the heart. It is unlikely that it will ever become quite the rage that it was in the last quarter of the nineteenth century when the two-wheeler was looked upon as a new and marvelous invention. Many songs were written to the wonderful velocipede and some had a rhythm that could easily be hummed as huge groups of avid cyclists pedalled their way through parks and country roads.

The earliest ancestor of the modern bicycle was a two-wheeled vehicle without pedals that was called the "hobby horse" or "draisine." This type of bicycle was pushed along the ground with one's feet, and although it probably beat walking it wasn't terribly popular. The "hobby horse" was probably invented as early as 1690, but it didn't catch on until a model was invented in Paris by Baron Karl von Drais in 1816. A Scottish blacksmith is credited with inventing the first bicycle with pedals in 1839 and the next important development came in 1862 when Pierre Michaux and Pierre Lallement invented the velocipede, a "hobby horse" with foot pedals connected to the front axle that looked much like our modern tricycles. The ride was said to have been "bone-shaking."

The configuration of the velocipede changed as innovators attempted to work out a cycle with more speed and a more comfortable ride. The front wheels became larger than those in the rear, and at first the cyclist sat almost directly over the front wheel, which in some cases was as large as sixty inches. By 1872 the high-wheel velocipede, or "ordinary," was equipped with ball bearings, wire wheels, and solid rubber tires. The cycle was still difficult to operate and required a pair of long legs.

In 1879 a British inventor, H. J. Lawson, overcame these disadvantages with the invention of the safety bicycle, and this vehicle was improved upon by J. K. Starley. Starley's version, which first appeared in 1885, was very like our modern bicycles with two wheels of the same size. The next remarkable discoveries in connection with bicycles were air-filled tires which were standard equipment by 1893 and the coaster brake, which was put on bikes in 1898. Innovations in bicycle manufacturing were later adapted by automobile makers and among these devices were knee action, variable-speed transmissions, free-wheeling, the drive shaft, and ball bearings.

It was little wonder that the developments in the bicycle industry inspired so many songs. Cycling became a widespread organized sport in the United States, clubs were formed, and each had its own song that could be sung in unison by a cycling group at least when it coasted *downhill*. "Velocipedia" is an early cycling song, published in 1868, and the cover is important in that it illustrates four vignettes with a variety of the kinds of cycles then being used. One young lady is riding a three-wheeler, while another rides one-handedly while she balances a milk can on her head with the other.

It is possible to imagine the Mercury Bi Club of New York riding through the streets to the lilting words of "Mister Tobias Isaias Elias," a song dedicated especially to them. "Bicycle Glide," which was "respectfully dedicated to the Philadelphia Bicycle Club," was written in 1880, and the cover shows a cyclist taking a leisurely ride along the Schuylkill River while a locomotive passes on a bridge overhead. "Knights of the Wheel Schottische" was written for the Albany Bicycle Club in 1884, and the cyclist on the cover is wearing a chestful of ribbons that one might assume were awarded for his ability to stay on what looks like an impossible vehicle.

The New Orleans Bicycle Club had its own "Bicycle March," as did clubs all over the country. The men and women who had special talents for riding became heroes. A good collectors' item is "The Cycle King" with a photograph of Eddie "Cannon" Bald draped discreetly in the American flag. Bald, also known as the White Flyer, was the cycle champion of 1895.

Cycling had really taken the country by storm by the end of the century, and in 1892 the greatest of all the cycle songs was published. Harry Dacre wrote the words and music to "Daisy Bell," better known as "Bicycle Built for Two." Dacre, who was English, came to America with his own bicycle and was charged duty for it. His friend said, "It's lucky you didn't bring a bicycle built for two, otherwise you'd have to pay double duty." The phrase stuck in Dacre's head, and he wrote his famous song about it. The song was first performed in London, where it was an immediate hit, and it was introduced in this country by Tony Pastor in his own music hall in New York. Jennie Lindsay also made the song popular when she performed it at the Atlantic Gardens on the Bowery.

By the mid-nineteenth century ice skating was a passion in all areas of the United States where the winter season was long enough and cold enough. In addition to outdoor skating some indoor rinks were built, and since most of these have long since disappeared, the pictures on the covers of sheet music are often the only record we have of these remarkably engineered indoor ponds. The engraving by Forbinger & Co. of Cincinnati of the Detroit Skating Rink found on the cover of "Rink Waltz" (1865) is both historically and artistically important. The building shown is remarkable in that there were no interior support beams, which left a large clear space for the skaters.

The Krebs & Bros. lithograph on "The Central Skating Park Polka," showing the park in Pittsburgh in 1865, is important to collectors of transportation items as well as those who collect sporting prints. The park seems to have been accessible both by horse-drawn trolley and train. The view of the trolley in the foreground is especially clear, and the rink house is a perfect example of mid-nineteenth-century architecture.

While ice-skating had been a necessary means of transportation in some areas of Europe for many years, it was not until the invention of the steel skate in 1850 that it became a popular sport as well. In the late nineteenth century roller skates were a new invention. The first skates with wooden wheels were invented by J. L. Plimpton of New York in 1863. Skates with pin bearings came next, and these were followed in 1883 by ball-bearing roller skates. It did not take Americans long to see the possibilities of developing roller skating as an indoor sport that could be enjoyed by children and adults. Rinks were built, the sport became extremely popular, and many songs were written about it. An especially good roller skating item is "McGinty the King of the Rink," which has an amusing picture on its cover.

By the middle of the nineteenth century it had already become customary for songs to be written in honor of any athletic endeavor, and a relatively early item of this type is "Athletic Waltz," composed and dedicated to John

Sheridan, Esq., (professor of gymnastics) and the athletes of Boston. The Thayer lithograph of 1844 shows an interior of a gymnasium, with men boxing, fencing, and working out on a variety of gymnasium apparatus which doesn't appear to be too different from modern equipment.

Bowling fell into disrepute at the beginning of this century before it was again revived as a wholesome sport open to men and women. In 1847 it was considered a "gentleman's sport" in which women were not allowed to indulge. "The Knickerbocker Saloon" shows the interior of an elegant bowling alley in which gentlemen could engage in a little exercise in their shirtsleeves.

From the cover of the "Brunswick Polka Mazurka," a piece dedicated to J. M. Brunswick, proprietor of billiard parlors, one can see that those establishments were originally gentlemanly palaces of pleasure. The picture on the cover, by the Chicago Lithograph Company, shows a palatial interior with a multitude of tables. Especially amusing are the "arms" below the picture with billiard balls and crossed cues.

According to the cover of "The Steeple Chase Two Step," San Franciscans were not without their sources of amusement in the late nineteenth century. Adults and children could ride over "hills" and "obstacles" in that city's Central Park.

Individual accomplishment in a sport was duly rewarded in song. Note the 1871 song, "The Merriest Girl in the Village," dedicated to Miss Abbie E. Barlow, whose game seemed to have been croquet. Miss Barlow's accomplishments would have been long forgotten were it not for an admiring composer and lyricist.

Of all the athletic games that started in the nineteenth century none has caught on nor lasted as long as baseball, which became our national sport. The origins of the game are still being disputed. There is a legend that it was invented by Abner Doubleday of Cooperstown, New York, in 1839, but the facts are that baseball is descended from an old English game called "rounders" and from cricket. From these two games there developed a game called "town ball" which was well known in New England by 1830. It was played on a square field at the corners of which were posts serving as bases. The first team scoring a hundred points won the game.

A man named Alexander Cartwright, a draftsman and surveyor by trade, laid out what is essentially the modern baseball field and drew up rules for the New York Knickerbocker Club in 1845. The Knickerbockers are considered to be the first official ball club in the United States, and they played their first game on Cartwright's Field in June 1846 in Hoboken, New Jersey. The Knicks lost, 23 to 1, to the New York Nine.

The Civil War is largely responsible for the widespread popularity of baseball in the United States. The game became a popular form of amusement for the soldiers in camp. After the war the soldiers carried the game to all parts of the country, and teams sprang up everywhere. The teams inspired the composition of many songs and poems.

An especially early baseball item is "The Red Stockings," dedicated in

1869 to the "ladies of Cincinnati." The polka, schottische, and march has a cover decorated with portraits of the team and a pitcher in contemporary uniform. The heroes of the diamond have not been ignored throughout the history of baseball by songwriters, and Ty Cobb, Babe Ruth, and recently, Hank Aaron, have all had songs written about them.

There are hundreds of old songs with American sports history as the subject, and a collector can specialize in any single sport that appeals. The earliest songs and musical pieces have lithographed covers that give us a vivid picture of the beginnings of many of our national pastimes.

Late minstrel item, 1890, is about racetrack betting.

Earliest railroad music sheet. Published by John Cole, Baltimore, 1828.

Music cover showing *Great Western* on voyage from Bristol, England, to New York. Lithograph by Nathaniel Currier, ca. 1840.

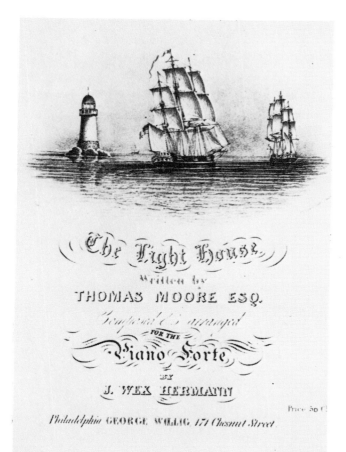

"The Light House," written by Thomas Moore. Duval lithograph. Published by George Willig, Baltimore, 1841.

Early balloon cover. P. Duval lithograph, Philadelphia, no date.

Popular song about flying, 1911.

Song written in 1924 became "official" song played everywhere when Lindbergh returned from his famous Atlantic flight.

One of at least a hundred songs written in honor of Lindbergh's famous flight in 1927.

Automobiling song was great hit in 1913.

Cycling song written in 1868.

Music written for the Philadelphia Bicycle Club in 1880.

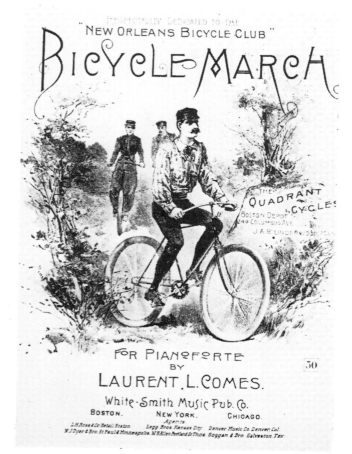

Music written for New Orleans Bicycle Club, 1892.

What the well-dressed woman cyclist wore in 1890.

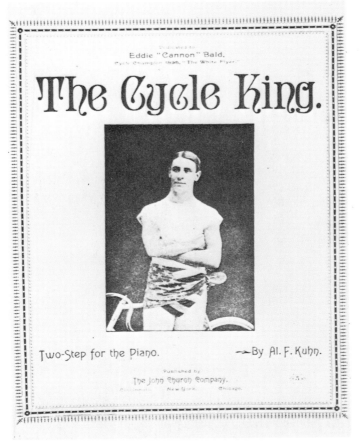

Cycling hero dressed in American flag, 1896.

Views of Detroit skating rink in 1865.

Skating park in Pittsburgh, 1865.

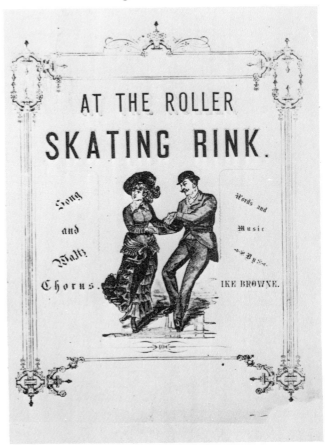

Roller-skating music, 1884.

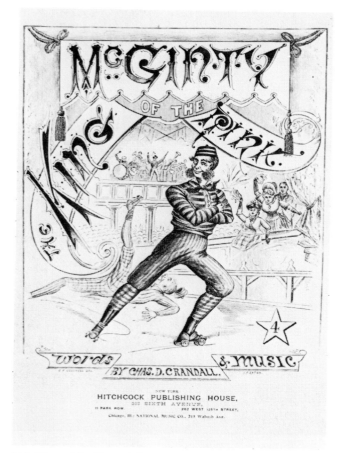

"McGinty, The King of the Rink," 1884.

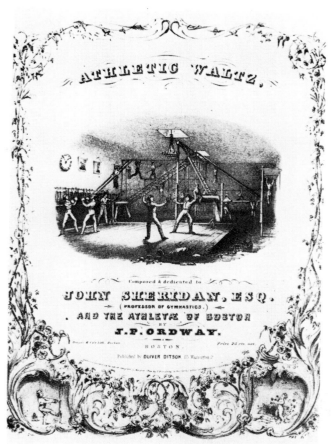

Early view of athletic club in Boston, 1844. Thayer & Co. lithograph.

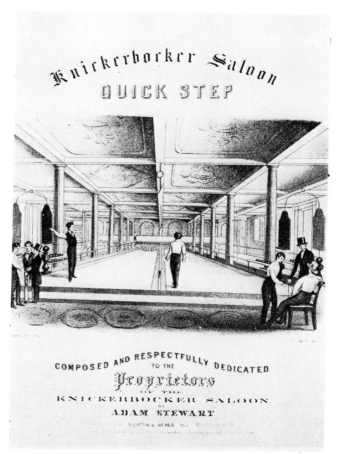

Bowling, 1840-style. Lithograph by W. Sharp & Co., Boston.

Cover showing interior of billiard parlor, 1869. Chicago Lithographing Company.

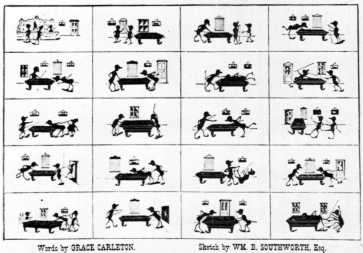

"Billiards on the Brain" with both "ladies' version" and "gentlemen's version." Published in New York in 1875.

San Francisco diversion in 1890s was steeplechase.

Music written for game of croquet in 1871. J. H. Bufford lithograph, Boston.

Early baseball music dedicated "to the ladies of Cincinnati," 1869.

Baseball song, Monsch lithograph, Cincinnati, 1877.

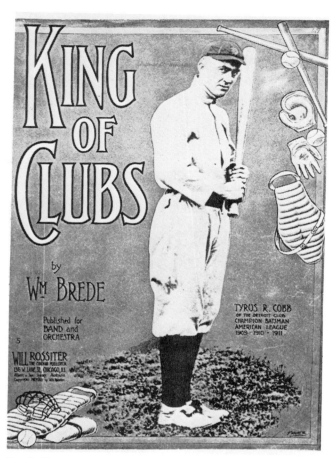

Baseball song written for Ty Cobb, 1912.

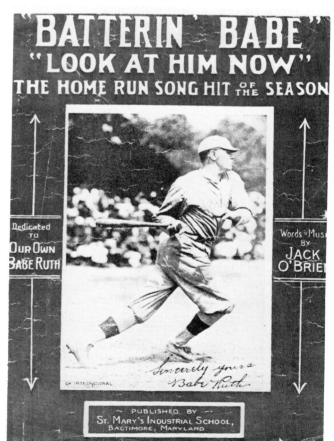

"Batterin' Babe," 1927.

More recent baseball song will become collector's item. Song for Hank Aaron, 1973.

"EVENT" MUSIC SHEETS OF THE NINETEENTH CENTURY

Throughout the nineteenth century songwriters seemed to wait for something to happen about which they could compose a work that might appeal to the public. All of these rather specialized songs fit rather broadly into a category known as "event" songs. The songs and musical pieces were written for public heroes, national or local tragedy or disaster, the construction of a new building or other architectural wonder such as the opening of the Brooklyn Bridge, the gold rush to California, and the discovery that oil could be taken from America's rich soil. Together, the sheet music covers and the songs represent many of the important developments throughout nineteenth-century America.

"Event" songs usually are rather short-lived, and often the lyrics and melody are less than memorable. Tragic fires were so common in the nineteenth century that they provided many composers with material for music and sad lyrics. There are hundreds of collectors of "tragedy" music today, and when the songs are not specific concerning *which* fire, shipwreck, or other specific occurrence they tell of they are of less interest than the ballads that sadly describe the happenings with which even today's historians are familiar.

For those who collect nineteenth- and early twentieth-century sheet music there is a wealth of history in the event songs of the period. Many of these songs were of purely local interest and point out how scattered and isolated the music publishing business really was in the period before New York became the music publishing center of the United States. If a local school was built and dedicated, a new march, two-step, or schottische would be written and taken to the nearest lithographer to be printed up in time for the dedication. Since this was the period before million-copy sellers, the composer didn't expect more than a few dollars for these purely local efforts, and often he would write his music to order for a flat fee.

Event music is collected, not for the music or lyrics (where they exist), but for the covers that represent the country's history of the nineteenth century. Any event that was important enough to inspire the composition of musical pieces could usually be suitably illustrated, and the artists who designed covers for the lithographers and printers of the nineteenth century could find inspiration in many of the event songs. Wrecked ships, burning buildings, and any other aptly described disaster were appealing subjects for sheet music covers. Because many of these pieces of music were not published in very large quantity they are difficult to find today. Furthermore, there are collectors of other specialized subjects who search for event songs in their specialty. For instance, the many collectors of marine antiques search for all music having to do with ships and sea disasters.

The sad song, or ballad, could be given a splendid workout when a disaster occurred, and many of the disaster songs of the earlier part of the nineteenth century predicted the later popularity of the dramatic ballads that appeared in great number towards the end of the century. The songwriters let few national or local events go by without at least one song or musical piece that would commemorate it.

Tragedies and disasters that were important enough to be reported in the news inspired writers of popular "event" music. The more tragic the story, the better the possibility that the song would be a hit. Really "tragic" would be the involvement of little children in some hideous tale of disaster, and while the events themselves were forgotten with time, the songs written for them linger on even though they are far from memorable themselves.

Apparently during the nineteenth century it was customary to stand around the piano in the parlor and sing of burning ships and buildings, wrecked ships (preferably with all hands lost), floods, earthquakes, murders, and even kidnappings. Today, it is difficult to find public records of some of the tragic happenings that inspired these sad songs, but at the time they were written the latest terrible disaster was on everyone's tongue.

There are today hundreds of fire-fighting buffs, and their special interest is song covers that have lithographs, preferably hand-colored, of firefighters of the nineteenth century and their equipment. "Homeless To Night," written in 1872, shows on its cover two waifs who have obviously been burned out of an enormous building that somewhat resembles a castle complete with towers and crenelated roof. A pumper is at work in the background in the obviously futile effort of bringing the raging fire under control.

We have already seen that the songwriters of America did not let a presidential assassination go by without turning out in record time the appropriate number of songs about the tragedy. Disaster collectors also search for other related material such as an early copy of "Our American Cousin Polka," written about the play Lincoln was attending when he was shot.

A kidnapping in 1874 was inspiration for songwriters to compose "Bring

Back Our Darling." Nobody did, and the child was never heard from again.

A particularly sad song and one that must have had great sentimental impact is "His Sacrifice," the story of a crippled newsboy from Gary, Indiana, Billy Rugh, who offered his skin for a grafting operation needed for a young girl. The operation was a success and the girl lived, but poor Rugh died. On the cover of the song is a photograph of the unfortunate Billy Rugh showing his crippled leg and his crutch. There is also a picture of the crowd that attended the magnificent funeral procession given to the boy.

Pure tragedy was one cause for writing a song, but when disaster could be mixed with scandal of national interest, chances for a song's success were even better. "For the Sake of Wife and Home" was billed as the Song Sensation of the Year in 1913, and the scandal that inspired the song was certainly a sensation. On the cover of the song is a large portrait of Harry Thaw, who murdered architect Stanford White, a member of the prestigious architectural firm of McKim, Mead, and White. He helped design, among other buildings, the New York Public Library, the old Madison Square Garden, and New York City's Washington Arch. Harry Thaw, who certainly appears to be mild-mannered enough, was driven to a crime of passion when he suspected White of carrying on with his wife, the actress Evelyn Nesbitt. Thaw was a Pittsburgh millionaire, and the trial was reported in all its gory details. The song, sympathetic to Thaw, undoubtedly ran its course as a hit when the news of the scandal was at its height.

If America liked to sing about its tragedies and disasters, there was plenty of opportunity to do it during the Great Depression of the 1930s. The songs that came from that era were most often of the "cheer up" variety, but many others went straight to the heart of the problem. The Rodgers and Hart classic, "Ten Cents a Dance," Lew Brown and Ray Henderson's "Life Is Just a Bowl of Cherries," Billy Rose and Mort Dixon's "I Found a Million Dollar Baby—In a Five and Ten Cent Store," and E. Y. Harburg and Jay Gorney's "Brother, Can You Spare a Dime?" could not have been written at any other time. There were many more songs from that era that haven't become standards such as "(Old Man Hard Times) Make Way for Kid Prosperity." In 1930 the writer Sam Coslow was being overly optimistic.

Songs were also written to the men whose job it was to protect country, home, life, and limb. In addition to firemen, local militia and even the police of the nineteenth century all had their own musical pieces written for them. Songwriters were able to provide appropriate music for every occasion and purpose. Nobody can claim that America's heroes went unsung.

A desirable type of what might be called "architectural music" is the item that has a lithograph of the music store or "saloon" on the cover. This was a form of self-advertising, but it gives us an image today of what the streets, buildings, and shops looked like in the nineteenth century, and these items are important especially to sheet music collectors.

Schools and colleges sprang up at a rapid rate, and music was written to celebrate this educational progress. One remarkable architectural wonder of the century was the construction and completion of the Brooklyn Bridge in

New York. The music written to help celebrate the opening festivities of the bridge in 1883 was "The 19th Century Wonder March." The cover has a fine illustration of the bridge as it appeared when just finished.

Hotels, spas, churches, parks, and all of the many expositions and fairs of the century were honored by the composers. The "Grand Exposition March," dedicated to Potter Palmer, president, was written for the Inter-State Industrial Exposition of 1873, which was held in Chicago.

When the one hundredth birthday of the nation was celebrated with the building of a gigantic exposition in Philadelphia, the composers went to work to write songs dedicated to almost every building that made up the great complex of architectural and mechanical wonders. The fair was, of course, a huge year-long success, and while the nation talked of nothing else, the composers busily turned out celebration music.

Official engravings of each point of interest at the exposition were made and used in a variety of ways. The major use of these pictures was as advertising and for illustrating the souvenir books that could be purchased for those fortunate enough to attend to take away with them to show the folks back home what they had missed. The official engravings were also used as cover decoration on the many musical pieces that were used to celebrate the opening and dedication of each building. For the time, of course, these buildings were considered the architecture of the future and since most of the buildings were to be torn down at the end of the centennial, the official engravings are the only record that exists.

One piece of centennial music illustrated here is unique in that it might be the only music written especially for an engine. The Corliss engine was situated in Machinery Hall at the centennial exposition, and it provided the power for the entire complex. The engine was nominally intended to provide 1,500 horse power, but was capable of providing 2,500 if necessary. Fortunately, the engine was never taxed to its limit, but the huge contraption was considered one of the wonders of the entire exposition and was visited with some regularity. The height of the Corliss engine was thirty-nine feet, and every part of it was accessible by means of iron staircases and balconies. To many visitors an inspection of the huge machine was the high point of their trip to Philadelphia, and it is likely that many bought copies of "The Corliss Engine Characteristic Grand March" to take home and play on their pianos.

There are many pieces of music written for the ships that took the California settlers to their new home, but all of this music was published in other parts of the country. The earliest known item of music to have been published in California is "The California Pioneers," a song published and sold by Atwill & Co., which was copyrighted on March 19, 1852. The lithographer and artist was Quirot & Co. of San Francisco. The words and music were written by Dr. M. A. Richter. All early California music is considered to be worth collecting, but this song with its cover showing two men dressed in buckskin is the song most in demand by collectors who specialize in items of the old West.

Not unlike the gold rush to California a decade earlier was the rush to cash in on "black gold." The discovery that precious oil could be extracted from beneath the earth's surface was a cause for rejoicing and for the writing of songs, many of them of a humorous nature. No one knows for certain who first had the idea of drilling for oil, but a New York lawyer, George H. Bissell, was largely responsible for the drilling of the first well that started the petroleum industry in the United States.

Bissell bought land that had seepages on Oil Creek near Titusville, in western Pennsylvania. He organized the Pennsylvania Rock Oil Company, which was later reorganized as the Seneca Oil Company. The latter firm drilled the land purchased by Bissell. The man who was sent to supervise the drilling was a retired railway conductor, Edwin L. Drake, who selected the site on which the first well would be drilled. Drake erected a wooden tower which was used to raise or lower the drilling tools. He solved the problem of cave-ins by lining the wall of the hole with sections of pipe.

In August 1859 oil was struck at Drake's well at a depth of sixty-nine and a half feet, and the well flowed at the rate of eight to ten barrels a day. Since crude oil was then selling for twenty dollars a barrel, everyone involved in the venture was well rewarded. The success of this well did not go unnoticed by the American press and public, and the search for oil by citizens from all parts of the country began. The country became petroleum-crazed, and the discovery of great gushers in many states, including Ohio, Oklahoma, Texas, and California, brought even more speculators who started boom towns wherever a gusher was brought in. "Have you struck Ile?" was considered a logical question for the poor gaunt man on the cover of a piece of sheet music to ask the fat man who holds a stack of thousand-dollar bills and a huge sack of money.

One songwriter wrote:

> Petroleum is king of the million
> With greenbacks enough at command
> To pay off the debt of the nation
> And buy all the cotton at hand.

The songsters could not foresee that petroleum would remain "king of the million" for more than a hundred years.

The nation was not without its entertainment events in the mid-nineteenth century. Many performers toured the country, and some were brought from Europe to America and promoted in advance in order to insure full houses wherever they went. It should come as no surprise that there are many examples of sheet music that represent various aspects of the career of Phineas Taylor Barnum, nineteenth-century America's greatest showman. One musical piece illustrated in this chapter shows Barnum before he became a circus owner. Today, a "National Poultry Show" might not inspire the composition of a polka or any other special music, but in the mid-nineteenth century such a show, especially if Barnum was in charge, was noteworthy. It is interesting that Barnum was promoting poultry before he graduated to human freaks.

In 1842 Barnum purchased the American Museum in New York City, and around the same time he discovered Charles S. Stratton, a midget from Bridgeport, Connecticut. Barnum named his little man "Tom Thumb" and exhibited him and his equally tiny wife all over the world. The marriage of Tom Thumb was an extravaganza produced in New York by the great promoter, and the wedding and every subsequent event in the lives of the midget couple were recorded in newspapers around the world. It was inevitable that special songs would be written to record the famous marriage and the participants.

Another well-known promotion of Barnum's was the concert tour he arranged for Jenny (Johanna Maria) Lind, the "Swedish Nightingale," in 1850–51. Miss Lind had a pure, sweet voice with great power and range and made her operatic debut in 1838, after which she sang in Paris and in the cities of Germany. She toured England in 1847–48 and made her last operatic appearance in 1849. She was brought to the United States preceded in true Barnum style by widespread publicity. The tour was an enormous success.

Among the many songs written for Miss Lind were "Jenny Lind's (Bird) Song," which has a beautifully illustrated cover with birds in their natural plumage; "Ossian's Serenade," on the cover of which is an illustration of P. T. Barnum introducing Jenny Lind to Ossian E. Dodge, the Boston vocalist and purchaser of a $625 ticket to Miss Lind's first concert in Boston; "I've Left My Snow Clad Hills," which included the songs of Jenny Lind and is illustrated by a chromolithograph of Jenny Lind after Baxter prints issued in England; Jenny Lind in "The Opera La Fille du Regiment" with a cover lithograph by Sarony of Miss Lind as "The Daughter of the Regiment"; and "Jenny Lind's Greeting to America" (illustrated in this chapter) with a full figure lithograph of the Swedish Nightingale by Brown.

Following her well-publicized tour of America Jenny Lind married a pianist and conductor and settled in England, where she sang in concerts and oratorios until 1870. Barnum, of course, went on to even bigger and better things. He became a member of the Connecticut Legislature in 1865 and in 1871 joined in partnership with W. C. Coup to form the first circus with its own railroad train.

Another nineteenth-century show business personality was William Frederick Cody, better known as Buffalo Bill. The nickname was given to him during a time when he was employed to kill buffalo to feed workers who were constructing the Kansas Pacific Railroad. Cody was a colorful figure who became chief of scouts for the Fifth U.S. Cavalry in 1868 and for the Third Cavalry in 1872. He took part in eleven expeditions and twelve fights against the Indians.

In 1869 E. C. Z. Judson wrote a dime novel about Cody, and three years later he persuaded Cody to appear in a play, *Scouts of the Prairie*. This started a long and lucrative career for Cody that fluctuated according to the season between winters on the stage and summers as an Indian scout.

Buffalo Bill had further adventures at the frontier in the Sioux War of 1876 when he killed an Indian leader and rescued two messengers. He became a hero.

It wasn't until 1883 that Cody started his Wild West exhibition of frontier life. The show included Indians, cowboys, soldiers, the Deadwood coach, the Pony Express, and reenactments of historic events, sometimes by the original participants. The show attracted world-wide attention and Cody and his troupe were invited to perform for Queen Victoria's Jubilee in 1887. In all, Cody's Wild West show toured Europe and America for more than thirty years and many songs were written especially for these performances. One musical piece was "Sharpshooter's March—As Played on the Grounds of Buffalo Bill's Wild West Show in 1894." By 1911, when "Buffalo Bill's Farewell" was written, photographs were being used on music sheet covers and we can see the actor-hero in all his western regalia.

Four areas of the arts came together when music was specially written, illustrated, and then danced to. Some of the most charming music covers were designed to illustrate the great variety of dances that became popular in the nineteenth century. Many of the dances have since been forgotten, but their exotic names linger on in the lithographed and hand-painted covers.

The most collectible of the "dance" covers are those that represent the tour of the Austrian dancer, Fanny Elssler. Fanny was born in Vienna in 1810, and her father was the copyist and servant of the composer Joseph Haydn. Fanny danced in a children's company in her native city before she was seven, and from 1827 she toured all the cities of Europe. In 1841 she came to the United States and became enormously successful. She was a gifted dancer of great beauty and was received everywhere with great enthusiasm. She was especially known for her dancing of the Spanish Cachucha and other European folk dances, and she amassed a fortune and retired from the stage in 1851. Fanny's sister, Thérèse, was also a dancer, and an interesting Elssler item is "El Zapateado," which pictures Miss Elssler and her sister dancing in costume. The printing says "as danced by Mdes Fanny and Theodore Elssler," obviously an error on the part of the publisher of the song. Thérèse went on to become the morganatic wife of Prince Adalbert of Prussia, and Frederick William IV eventually gave her the title of Baroness von Barnim.

Dances such as "Valse en Tyrolienne," "La Cracovienne," and "El Zapateado" might mean little to us today, but in their day they were dances introduced by accomplished soloists and duetists who toured the country to great acclaim. The illustrators had an opportunity to design handsome covers of foreign folk costumes worn by the performers. An interesting cover is "The Celebrated Cancan Dance" as performed by Mlles. Morlacchi and Baretta, who are illustrated in a demure position in the Bufford lithograph. There is little connection between this dance as performed in 1868 and the more daring Cancan of the nineties.

Performed dancing (and social dancing) remained somewhat restrained until the first quarter of this century when the Charleston and all of its subsequent variations became popular. Sheet music related to well-known dancers is collected by those who are interested in the history and development of the dance as an art form in America. The covers are often colorful and artistic and they display an interesting variety of theatrical costumes used in the nineteenth century. However, the Elssler covers are the most in demand by today's dance music collectors.

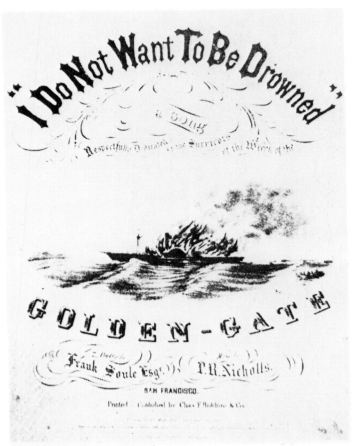

"Disaster" music with cover showing wreck of the *Golden-Gate.* Geo. H. Butler lithograph, San Francisco, 1862.

"Fireman's Song." T. Moore lithograph, Boston, 1836.

Song about tragic fire in 1872.

Song about tragic kidnapping in 1874. Child was never found.

"Disaster" song written for victims of flood, 1913.

Song about newsboy who sacrificed his life for little girl in Gary, Indiana.

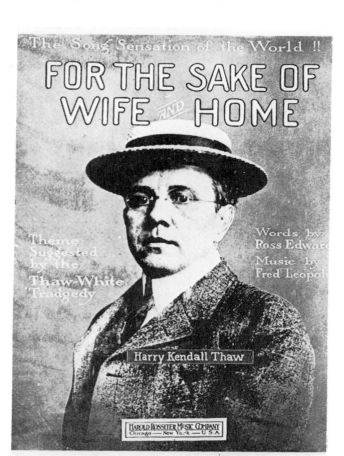

Song about the Thaw-White scandal of 1913.

Music composed in honor of the police reserves, 1918, has cover illustration by Harrison Fisher.

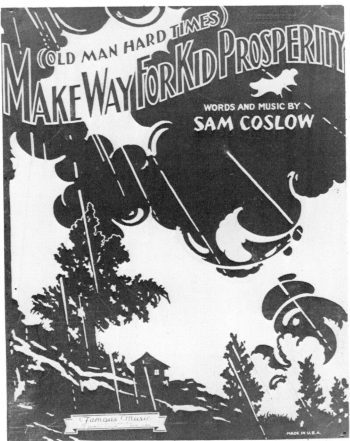

Depression song has interesting silhouette cover in style of 1930.

Song written about great oil boom in 1865. Composer listed inside is "O.I.L. Wells." Ehrgott, Forbiger, & Co. lithograph, Cincinnati.

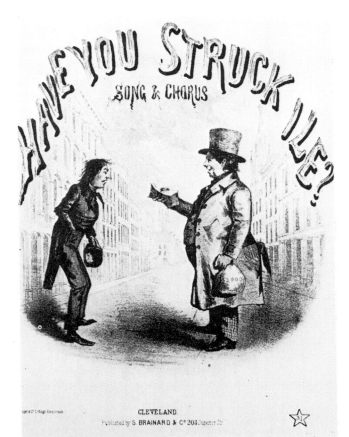

"Have You Struck Ile?" has comic cover lithograph by Ehrgott, Forbiger, & Co., Cincinnati, 1865.

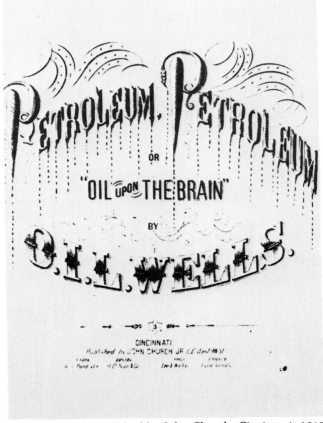

Petroleum song published by John Church, Cincinnati, 1865.

Polka, published in 1853, has lithograph of Fifth Avenue Hotel, New York.

"Point Breeze Park," schottische, T. Sinclair lithograph, Philadelphia, 1861.

Music written for dedication of Brooklyn Bridge, May 24, 1883.

CROTON WATER CELEBRATION 1842

Music written for opening of Croton Aqueduct, City Hall
Park, New York, 1842.

GRAND EXPOSITION MARCH.

Lithograph by W. W. Royington shows building of the Inter-
State Industrial Exposition of Chicago, 1873.

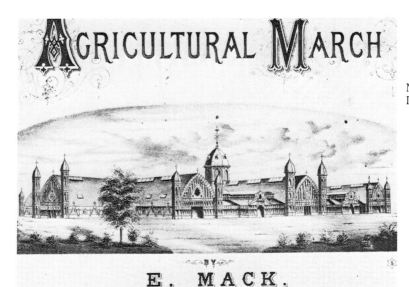

March for Agricultural Hall, Centennial Exposition, Philadelphia, 1875.

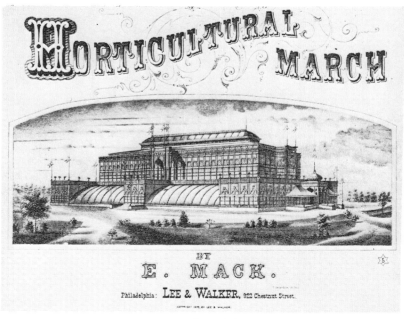

Horticultural Hall at Philadelphia exposition in 1875.

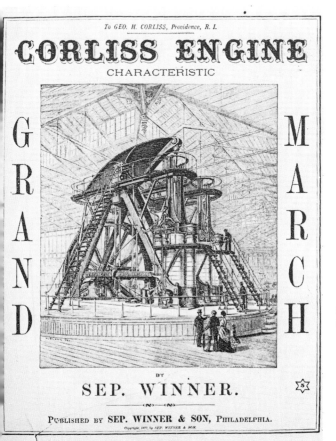

Music written to the great Corliss engine of the centennial celebration in Philadelphia, 1875.

Great P. T. Barnum as he looked in 1854.

Jenny Lind song, E. Brown lithograph, New York, 1850.

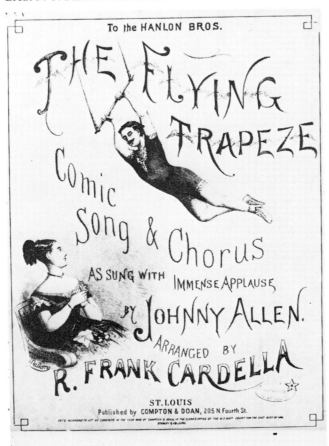

The writer of this song is not known, but it was written in 1868 and was popularized in vaudeville in the 1870s by Johnny Allen.

Music written for Buffalo Bill Cody in 1894.

LA CACHUCHA.

AS DANCED BY

MAD:lle FANNY ELSSLER.

"La Cachucha," dance music with illustration of Fanny Elssler. Fleetwoods lithograph, New York, 1840.

MALVINA

VALSE EN TYROLIENNE.
composée pour le Piano
et dediée à
MADEMOISELLE ELISABETH RICHARDS
par
GUSTAVE BLESSNER.

"Malvina" dance cover. Duval lithograph, Philadelphia, 1843.

JULLIEN'S ORIGINAL,

CORLITZA.
ARRANGED FOR THE
PIANO FORTE.

BOSTON:
Published by OLIVER DITSON, 115 Washington St.

"Corlitza" dance cover. H. W. Thayer & Co. lithograph, 1850.

The celebrated
CANCAN DANCE

EXECUTED BY
M:lle MORLACCHI AND BARETTA.

BOSTON:
Published by OLIVER DITSON & CO. 277 Washington St.

Cancan dancers, 1868. Bufford lithograph, Boston.

"HOME, SWEET HOME," "OLD" SONGS, AND "MOTHER"

"Be it ever so humble" there is no collectors' item like a first American edition of "Home, Sweet Home." The song is probably the best known of all ballads in the English language and certainly one of the most sentimental. It was written by John Howard Payne (words) and Sir Henry Rowley Bishop (music) in 1823. Payne was a descendant of Robert Treat Payne, one of the signers of the Declaration of Independence and had gone to Europe as a young man, where he became stranded in Paris. He was offered a job in London by Charles Kemble, manager of the Covent Garden Theatre, who asked Payne to adapt the French play *Clari* to an opera. *Clari*, or *Maid of Milan*, was first performed on May 8, 1823, and "Home, Sweet Home" was a part of the score. It was first sung by Maria Tree at the end of the first act and was an instant success.

The song's popularity spread first through London, then England, and finally throughout the whole Western world. Its composer, Bishop, was knighted by Queen Victoria in 1842 for composing the melody. For his part, Payne said that he only wrote what was in his heart; that he had become homesick and yearned for America and his family.

Even though "Home, Sweet Home" was first introduced by Maria Tree, the song was an enormous success for other performers as well. Kitty Stephens introduced it at the York and Birmingham festivals in 1832, and the wife of the composer, Mme. Anne Bishop, a noted concert singer, made it a part of her repertoire. However, the song's great fame came mainly when two singers, Jenny Lind and Adelina Patti, added it to their concerts. Jenny Lind used it as her closing number in her American concerts, and one can assume that there wasn't a dry eye in the house by the time she finished.

Payne did not profit from his great hit, chiefly because there was no international copyright control in those days. He lamented once that there were times when he would be in one of the cities of Europe without a penny to his name and he would hear "Home, Sweet Home" being played by organ grinders in the streets. He did receive an honor, however, when he was invited to the White House by President Fillmore to hear Jenny Lind give a performance. Miss Lind sang her last number, "Home, Sweet Home," directly to Payne on that occasion. In addition, a statue was erected to Payne in Prospect Park, Brooklyn, New York, in 1873. Two benefit performances of *Clari* helped raise the funds.

Nobody seems to know for certain just where Payne's "Home, Sweet Home" really was. Three locations have been claimed as being Payne's place of birth, but the inspiration for the song is probably East Hampton, Long Island, where Payne's father lived during the lyricist's early childhood.

Just about every American music publisher cashed in on the popularity of "Home, Sweet Home." There is only one edition, however, that mentions John Howard Payne as having written the words, and that is the Oliver Ditson edition published in Boston. The earliest American edition was published by George Bacon in Philadelphia in 1823. Only a few of the nineteenth-century editions of the song have illustrated covers.

"Home, Sweet Home" had every requirement for a hit song in the early part of the nineteenth century. It was sentimental enough to bring tears to one's eyes, it had a memorable tune, and the words were easy to remember. There were hundreds of sentimental ballads written around the same time and the genre did not peter out for many years. Certainly, there can be found at least a faint resemblance between the earlier hymn to home and Stephen Foster's later (1851) "Old Folks at Home."

One peculiar aspect of songs from the first half of the nineteenth century was the tendency for the writers to keep a good thing going. The author of the ballad, "Good News From Home" also wrote "Sad News From Home." "The Old Arm Chair," written by Eliza Cook (words) and Henry Russell (music) in 1840 was an extremely popular ballad in its day:

> I love it, I love it,
> And who shall dare
> To chide me for loving
> That old arm chair.

The first hit, often referred to as the first "mammy" song in America, inspired an answer by lyricist John H. Warland and composer and performer S. C. Massett, which they called "Answer to the 'Old Arm Chair.'" Sadder than the original ballad, the narrator has now grown old and one can easily guess what piece of furniture she has chosen to die on.

There were a raft of "old" songs. The popularity of "The Old Maid" inspired an answer called "The Old Bachelor" and another called "The Old Beau."

There are, of course, hundreds of other sentimental ballads, one sadder than the other, from the nineteenth-century hit parade of songs. Most of them are collected today for their decorative covers.

Mother as a subject for song has been popular for many years, and one could collect "mother" songs until he had a rather large amount. Perhaps the best known of this genre is "M-o-t-h-e-r (a Word That Means the World to Me)" (words by Howard Johnson, music by Theodore F. Morse). This song, written in 1915, was a mammy song made popular by Sophie Tucker, who performed it in vaudeville.

An earlier ballad about mother was "Mother Was a Lady" (or, "If Jack Were Only Here"), written by Edward B. Marks and Joseph W. Stern in 1896. The popular ballad is said to have been inspired by an actual episode in a restaurant where two young men were harassing the waitress. In tears she exclaimed, "My mother was a lady! You wouldn't dare insult me if my brother Jack were only here!" The resultant ballad was introduced by Lottie Gibson at Proctor's Fifty-eighth Street Theatre in New York, and the performance helped launch a sheet music sale of over two million copies.

The turn-of-the-century ballad was so successful that other songwriters attempted to top it but to no avail. "That Wonderful Mother of Mine" and "Mammy O' Mine" were only two of the many "mammy" songs that were written in honor of maternity.

Many versions of this famous ballad were published since song was first written in 1823. This version was published in 1857.

"Sad News From Home," ballad published in 1854. Tappan & Bradford lithograph, Boston.

Ballad to a chair, Boston, 1840.

Answer to "The Old Arm Chair" was published in 1841. Thayer & Co. lithograph, Boston.

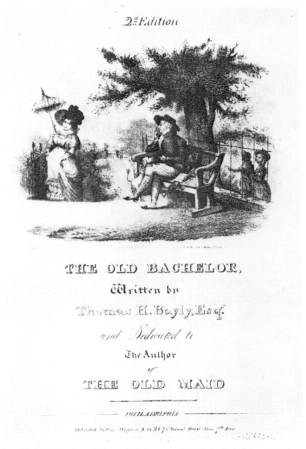

"The Old Bachelor," Duval lithograph, Philadelphia, 1834.

"The Old Man's Bride," ballad published in 1835. Duval lithograph, Philadelphia.

Turn-of-the-century "mammy" songs were written by the dozens.

A ballad to "mother" was usually a sure-fire hit in 1918.

SOCIAL ISSUES: WOMEN'S RIGHTS AND TEMPERANCE SONGS

Along with the slavery issue there were two other important social issues in the nineteenth century that inspired songwriters. In reality women's suffrage had nothing to do with the problem of temperance, and the two probably should never have been associated were it not for the fact that the women who went out for causes in those days believed both issues were equally important, and they probably also thought that the possibility of getting the vote could not be accomplished until they had rid the world of that Old Devil, Drink.

The fight for women's rights in the nineteenth century was a long uphill struggle, and the one woman who was most outspoken in her fight for suffrage seemed to have had more influence on the costume of her time and on popular music than she did on the unsympathetic male population of the period. Amelia Jenks Bloomer (1818–94) was a reformer who lectured on women's rights, and she might have been slightly more effective in that cause had she not also carried on many tirades against intemperance. Married to a newspaper editor, Dexter Bloomer, Amelia started the first publication in America by and for women in 1849. It was called *Lily*.

Although Mrs. Bloomer gave equal time in her lectures and articles to education, women's suffrage, slavery, and temperance, she is best known today as America's first women's liberation worker, and collectors now search for artifacts associated with that aspect of her life. For her lectures Mrs. Bloomer wore an ordinary bodice with a short skirt worn over full trousers elasticized at the ankles. This costume, thought at first to be "outrageous" by more conservative citizens, caught on by the 1850s, and there was much controversy over whether it was "proper." Evidently, the writers of popular songs thought that it was, and although they wrote about it, they did not poke fun at it. By 1851 the Bloomer costume had become enough of an issue to cause many popular songs to be written about it. Those with illustrated covers are a chronicle of the costume of the year.

"Bloomer Costume," dedicated to Mrs. Bloomer and the ladies in favor of the costume, has a Sarony and Major lithograph of a rather demure lady (probably Amelia Bloomer) dressed in the mode she made famous. Other musical pieces written that year that have illustrated covers are "The New Bloomer Schottische," "The Bloomer Waltz" with another Sarony and Major lithograph illustrating the "costume for summer," "The Bloomer Polka and Schottisch," illustrated by a Baltimore artist, A. Hoen, and "The Bloomer Quick Step" with yet another illustration by the same lithographer.

The style set by Mrs. Bloomer seems to have been rather short-lived, and the 1851 excitement died down almost as quickly as it started. The women's movement did not disappear, however, and it found another strong leader in Susan B. Anthony (1820–1906). Ms. Anthony's causes were similar to Mrs. Bloomer's, and she also tied the cause of temperance to her fight for women's rights. She helped organize the Woman's State Temperance Society in 1852 and worked closely with Elizabeth Cady Stanton on women's rights. Both women were active abolitionists and they also organized the Women's National Loyal League in 1853 to support the Union cause when hostilities commenced between North and South. The two women were among the first to advocate Negro suffrage.

After the war, Ms. Anthony devoted herself entirely to the woman's suffrage movement. She founded the National Woman's Suffrage Association in 1869 to work towards an amendment to the Constitution that would give women the right to vote.

An early and important suffrage item is illustrated here. The song, "We'll Show You When We Come to Vote," was written in 1869 and published in Toledo, Ohio. The cover engraving shows women casting their ballots at a ballot box labeled "For Ladies," and posted signs read "Susan B. Anthony for President," "Ladies Mass Meeting, Faneuil Hall, Boston," "For Governor of Massachusetts, Miss Lucy Stone," "For Governor of New York, Elizabeth Cady Stanton," "For Vice President, Mrs. Geo. F. Train," and "Down With Male Rule." Three dismayed gentlemen look on as women with babes in arms turn out to vote. Amelia Bloomer and Susan B. Anthony would not live long enough to see the nineteenth amendment finally pass in 1920. Nor could they have known that getting the right to vote would only be the beginning of the many issues that involve women's rights. However, the sheet music remains to give visual proof of the influence the crusading women had in their day.

It was women's influence that started the great temperance movement that had thousands of active advocates in the latter half of the nineteenth century. Not the least of these were the reformed drinkers who had taken the pledge. The movement was responsible for the adoption of prohibition laws in thirteen states before the Civil War. By the end of the war the law remained in effect in only four states, and in the next few decades the liquor business enjoyed a remarkable expansion in the country.

The dangers of overindulgence historically seem to have been something to sing about and the song, "Think and Smoke Tobacco" was already a "favorite old song" in 1836. The cover engraving illustrates the hazards of smoking and drinking too much. Under a picture of three men sitting at a table on which there are a bottle and glasses there is the inscription: "Ashes to ashes—earth to earth—dust to dust. When eyes are dim, ears deaf, teeth decayed, skin withered, breath tainted, pipes furred, knees trembling, hands fumbling, feet flailing, the sudden downfall of the fleshly house is near at hand."

Drunkenness has always been a problem in the United States, and as early as 1789, two hundred farmers in Litchfield, Connecticut, formed a temperance society at which they pledged, not for themselves, but to avoid giving strong drink to their workmen. Many church groups formed temperance societies throughout the nineteenth century and "moderation" was the earliest type of pledge. Gradually the movement advocated the abstinence from all alcoholic beverages, and at midcentury temperance workers began to demand legislation. The National Temperance Society was formed by organizing all state and local groups.

Prohibition came about at the same time that women's suffrage was passed. From the period between January 1920 until December 1933, when the Eighteenth Amendment was in effect, the country experienced that phenomenon known as Prohibition. During two centuries hundreds of songs have been written for and against John Barleycorn. Perhaps the most famous of these is "Father, Dear Father, Come Home," first published in 1914. The song was advertised as "the most effective Temperance Song ever published."

One of many musical pieces written in honor of Amelia Bloomer in 1851. A. Hoen & Co., Baltimore.

Suffragette song "We'll Show You When We Come to Vote." Publisher was W. W. Whitney, Toledo, Ohio, 1869.

Early song about mortality and the evils of smoking and drinking. Pendleton lithograph, Boston, 1836.

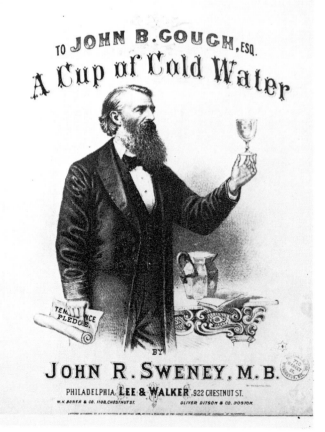

Temperance song published in 1873.

Most popular and most effective of all temperance songs was published first in 1914.

Drinking song of 1909.

Pre-Prohibition song published in 1919.

Favorite song of the drinking set since it was published in 1926.

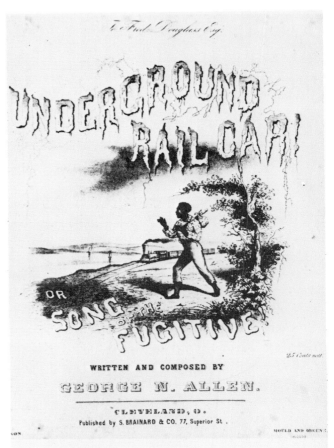

Abolitionist song published by S. Brainard & Co., Cleveland, 1854. O. Ditson lithograph.

MINSTREL MUSIC

We have already seen that the Negro was being depicted by white performers in blackface as early as 1824, when the song "Massa Georgee Washington and General Lafayette" was performed in New York. However, the song that had the most influence in establishing the nineteenth-century characterization of the black man on the American stage was first performed in 1828. This number, "Jim Crow," was a popular song-and-dance routine written and devised by Thomas "Daddy" Rice. It is regarded as having been responsible for the beginning of the American minstrel show.

One day while Rice was performing in Baltimore, so the story goes, he noticed an old crippled black man who walked with stumbled contortions. The man chanted gibberish to himself as he moved slowly along, and this scene so impressed Rice that he decided to include it in his act. He used tattered rags as a costume and did a shuffling dance, while singing gibberish verses which began:

> Wheel about an turn about
> An' do jis so;
> Eb'ry time I wheel about,
> I jump Jim Crow.

Rice danced grotesque postures and movements and on the words "jis so" he jumped as high as he could. The act was an enormous hit, and before the year was over blackface performers were using Rice's material all over the country. Impersonations of a stereotyped black became a permanent part of nineteenth-century popular theater. The term "Jim Crow," designating segregation, became a part of the American language. As late as 1917 Sigmund Romberg used the phrase in a song-and-dance operetta, *Maytime.*

Songs about blacks were a part of the American musical heritage from the late eighteenth century, and they were not always denigrating, although the genre, after the publication of "Jim Crow" around 1830, developed into a morass of black comedy put-downs that were sung and performed through the entire nineteenth century. The first Negro song on record was popular in 1769 and was titled "Dear Heart! What a Terrible Life Am I Led." It was sung by Lewis Hallam the Younger in Bickerstaffe's *The Padlock*. A song of 1793 was the "Desponding Negro" and in 1796 W. Norman of Boston published "I Sold a Guiltless Negro Boy." The earliest songs having to do with the black condition in America were sentimental and mostly sympathetic.

After the publication of "Jim Crow" the American minstrel gradually became a definite part of the national entertainment scene, and many less sympathetic songs having to do with blacks were performed and were considered to be totally acceptable. In addition, the songs sung about blacks were usually performed by white performers in blackface. Mr. Rice had started a trend in American popular music that couldn't be stopped. There followed a raft of dialect songs poking fun at the black population of America that was already beset with enough problems. Today's collectors of black-oriented music and illustrated covers do not specialize in this category for the same reasons that caused them to be written, published, and performed in the first place. If popular secular music is representative of our morals and virtues as well as our prejudices, then the entire history of the black song in American music is an important segment of the story if it is to be told truthfully.

In actuality the American minstrel had its roots in Britain where its antecedents were Negro characters and songs in dramas of the eighteenth century. The first performances in America of black dialect songs were given by Charles Mathews, an Englishman who came to this country in 1822. He became fascinated with American Negroes and attended their own theater in New York, collected dialects, and attended a black revivalist's meeting in Philadelphia. He helped to establish a stage tradition of presenting the stereotypical black character. Two separate types developed on the American stage: one, the tattered servant-type of low estate whose spirits nonetheless remained high; and the other, the urban dandy. Both types were grotesque comedic oversimplifications.

Little by little groups of white performers banded together into travelling shows and, covering their faces with burnt cork, they performed songs, skits, and dances that began to develop into a formula type of show. The Four Virginia Minstrels is the troupe that has been credited with putting together instruments associated with black musicians, and the combination of the banjo, violin, bone castanets, and tambourine became established as part of the American minstrel. Their performances in the early 1840s were billed as Ethiopian Concerts, and the first such show was given at the Masonic Temple in Boston on March 7, 1843. The dialect songs were called Ethiopian melodies.

The Jim Crow type of song spread rapidly across the country as groups

Cover designed by James McNeill Whistler of West Point. Sarony & Co. lithograph, hand-colored. New York, 1852.

"Old Ironsides," dedicated to Commodore Stewart. T. Sinclair & Son lithograph, Philadelphia.

"Atlantic Telegraph Polka," J. H. Bufford lithograph. Boston, 1868.

"Music of the Union," J. H. Bufford lithograph. Boston, 1861.

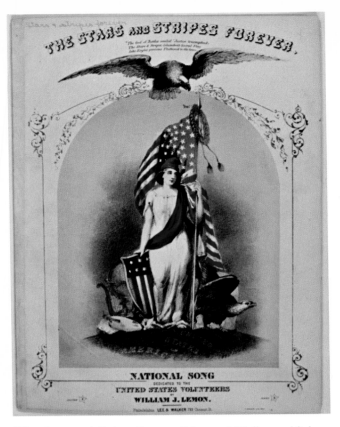

"The Stars and Stripes Forever," Lee and Walker publishers. Philadelphia, ca. 1860.

Winfield Scott, hero of Mexican War. J. H. Bufford lithograph. Boston.

"Chaplet," probably most beautiful music sheet ever published in United States. Flowers are notes and bees are sharps. R. H. Hobson and Pishey Thompson, Philadelphia. No date, but probably third quarter of nineteenth century.

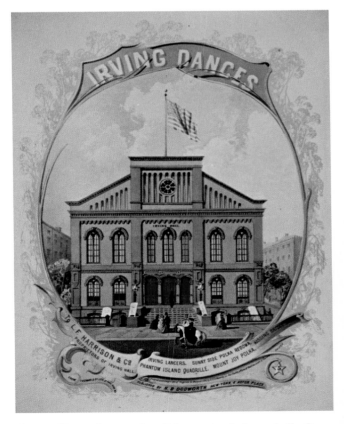

"Irving Dances" cover has lithograph of dance hall. Crow, Thomas, & Co. lithograph. New York, 1881.

"Mme. Anna Bishop," A. Fiot publisher. Philadelphia, 1848. Portrait done from daguerreotype.

"The Style of Thing," Thaddeus Firth publisher. New York, 1886.

"Little Red Riding Hood Galop," T. Sinclair lithograph. Philadelphia, ca. 1870.

"The Death of Minnehaha," J. H. Bufford lithograph. Boston, ca. 1860.

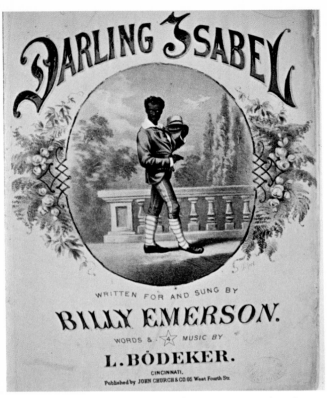

"Darling Isabel," song written and sung by minstrel performer Billy Emerson. John Church & Co., Cincinnati, 1877.

"The Easy Winners," one of Scott Joplin's earliest and best rags. Published by John Stark, St. Louis, 1901.

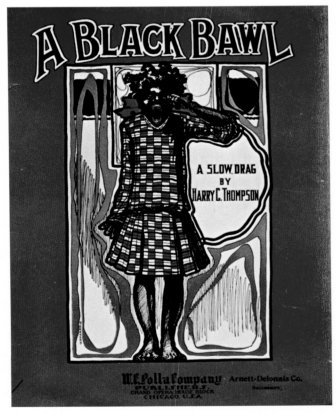

"Fig Leaf Rag" by Scott Joplin. Published by Stark Music Company, St. Louis and New York, 1908.

"A Black Bawl," a "slow drag" by Harry G. Thompson. W. C. Polla Company publishers, Chicago, 1905. Cover signed: H. Barnard.

"In My Merry Oldsmobile," M. Witmark & Sons publishers. New York, London, Chicago, 1905.

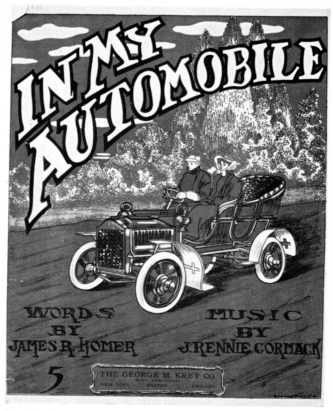

"In My Automobile," The George M. Krey Co. publishers. New York, Boston, Chicago, 1906.

"Cole 30 Flyer," automobile song of early 1900s.

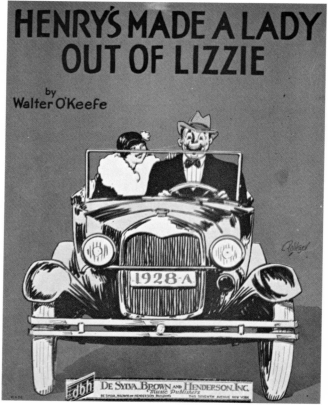

"Henry's Made a Lady out of Lizzie," published in 1928 by DeSylva, Brown, and Henderson.

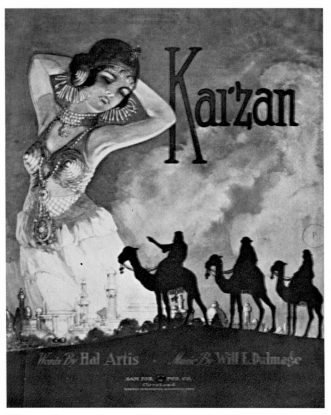

"Karzan," insignificant song with handsome cover published in 1919.

"That Night in Araby," song "inspired" by Rudolph Valentino movie, *The Son of the Sheik*, shortly before star's death in 1926.

Daring *Ziegfeld Follies* cover designed by Vargas in 1931.

Ziegfeld Follies song, "A Pretty Girl Is Like a Melody," had words and music by Irving Berlin and a cover design by Henry Clive. Song became theme song for all subsequent *Follies*.

Famous World War I song, "Over There," was written by George M. Cohan and has cover design by Norman Rockwell.

Rockwell also designed cover for less well-known World War I song, "Over Yonder Where the Lilies Grow."

Uncle Sam cover on World War I song, "You'll Be There."

Propaganda song to raise sympathy for bonuses to veterans after World War I.

"Brother, Can You Spare a Dime?" was one of most popular songs of Great Depression. First performed in 1932 in revue *Americana*.

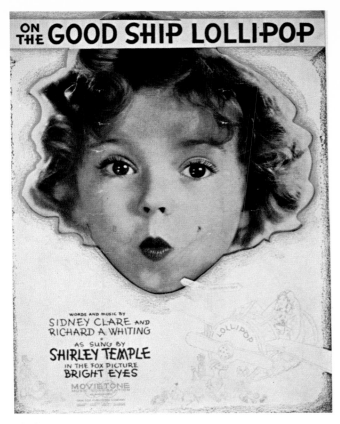

Shirley Temple on cover of one of her most famous songs, "On The Good Ship Lollipop" from film *Bright Eyes*, 1934.

Song that introduced Ginger Rogers and Fred Astaire to the movies. The song, an interpolation in the Cole Porter score for *Gay Divorcee*, was the first to win an Academy Award. RKO, 1934.

"For Me and My Gal" was written in 1917 and was featured in the MGM musical starring Judy Garland in 1942.

formed travelling minstrel shows. The better known and most successful of these were the Christy Minstrels, Bryant's Minstrels, and the Kentucky Rattlers. Others billed themselves as the Ethiopian Serenaders and the Guinea Minstrels.

Another song equally infamous as "Jim Crow" and as influential in black history of the nineteenth century is the song "Zip Coon." Its composer and lyricist are not known, but the song was a classic performed at thousands of minstrel shows after it first appeared in 1834. It was introduced at the Bowery Theatre in New York by minstrel Bob Farrell and was later a favorite of minstrel George Washington Dixon and other minstrels. "Zip Coon" was the epitome of the black dandy. Today the tune, probably derived from an old Irish melody, is more familiarly known as "Turkey in the Straw."

The lithographers of the sheet music for minstrel shows pictured the subjects of the song as they were depicted by the performers, as quasi-cartoon characters. The banjo "jigs" of the period, which became the ancestors, musically, of the later jazz and ragtime, were yet another element of the minstrels. This music was derived from black musicians who, if not able to perform in shows that came from their culture, since the performers were most often white men in burnt cork, were at least able to contribute their style of music.

The popularity and lucrativeness of the minstrel show were also responsible for some of America's most-played tunes that were written by Stephen Foster. Foster's greatest hit, "Old Folks at Home," was published under E. P. Christy's name, which Foster later realized was a mistake. The entire work of Stephen Foster is a collectible category in itself and first editions of any of his songs are in great demand.

The minstrel shows continued through most of the nineteenth century in one form or another and eventually became more diluted from the early form to become a variety and burlesque show. Black performers were finally hired towards the end of the century, often appearing in burnt cork make-up, and the travelling shows became larger and larger. One late minstrel performer who was black and contributed over seven hundred songs to the country's minstrel music was James A. Bland, who wrote "In the Evening By the Moonlight," "Oh, Dem Golden Slippers," "Carry Me Back to Old Virginny," and other still familiar tunes.

If the minstrel as a form of show business died out, the popularity of white performers playing in blackface did not. Vaudeville had its own dialect hits, and performers like Al Jolson and Eddie Cantor perpetuated the black stage image in the first quarter of this century. Meanwhile, the influences, both black and white, that met in the American minstrel show eventually combined to give us that most American of all music, jazz.

Song written in 1824 is generally thought to be the first of the blackface comic songs. Engraved by E. Riley, New York.

"Jim Crow" lithograph by Pendleton, New York, ca. 1829.

"Jim Crow," Geo. Willig, Jr., Baltimore, ca. 1830. This number was very popular on stage.

"Settin' on a Rail," J. L. Hewitt, New York, 1836–37.

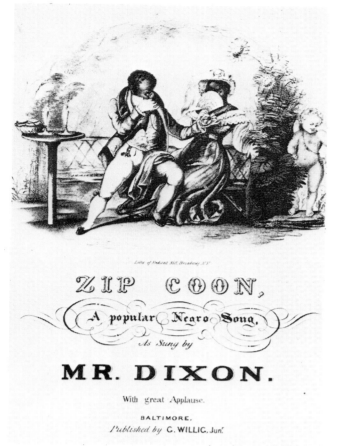

"Zip Coon," published by G. Willig, Baltimore, 1834.

Endicott lithograph on cover of "Zip Coon," New York, 1834. It is from this song that the stage stereotype of the black dandy arose.

Comic song for stage, published by Endicott, New York, 1836.

"Dandy Jim From Carolina," Endicott lithograph, New York, 1843.

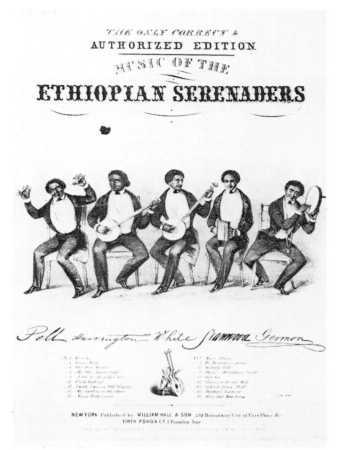

Early (1847) minstrel band showing typical instruments used: bones, banjo, accordion, and tambourine. William Hall & Son, publisher, New York, 1847.

Most famous of all minstrel artists was E. P. Christy. Oliver Ditson lithograph, Boston, 1847.

"Alabama Joe," Thayer lithograph, Boston, 1840.

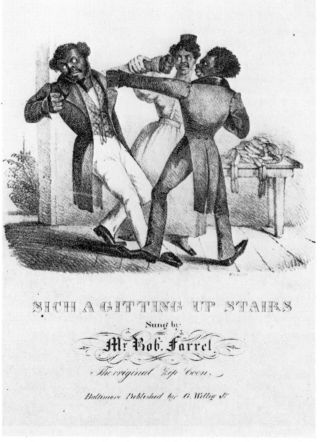

Popular stage number done in blackface by "the original Zip Coon." G. Willig, Jr., Baltimore.

SONGS OF STEPHEN FOSTER

The songs of Stephen Collins Foster are, along with Negro spirituals, the closest America has come to having a folksong literature of its own. There is little doubt that Foster's lyrics and music were influenced by the music of the blacks that he had observed during his childhood in Pennsylvania. It is thought that the greatest influence on his music was Sunday night services at the church he attended with the maid who lived with the Foster family for many years.

Foster was next to youngest of eleven children, and since his younger brother died in infancy Stephen was the baby of a very large family. Although there are many legends about his musical precocity, it is undoubtedly fact that his ability to make music was evident from a very early age. However, in the early nineteenth-century atmosphere in which Stephen Foster grew up schoolwork came before musical ability, especially for a boy, and he was given parental approval for not devoting more time to his music than he did to school. While at boarding school he did not practice until after eight o'clock, when his other work had been finished. He played the violin and flute and could pick out tunes on the piano. Piano playing, in Foster's day, was thought to be an accomplishment that should be pursued only by a woman. Certainly, the music business was not an occupation to be chosen for the son of a family that had an important social position in its community, even though its fortunes had fallen considerably and the family was often in debt during Foster's childhood.

Stephen Foster was born on the Fourth of July in Lawrenceville, Pennsylvania, in 1826. This was not just any Independence Day, but was the fiftieth anniversary of the country, and on Stephen's birthday John Adams and Thomas Jefferson died within hours of each other. Foster's only further connection with the presidency was that his sister Ann Eliza married the brother of President Buchanan.

Foster began his working career as a bookkeeper for his brother in Cincinnati. He worked at this job for three years, and he seems not to have been inefficient in his work even though he continued to write music during this period, and he spent much of his spare time in cultivating minstrel performers whom he hoped would plug his new songs in their performances. At the time this was the only way to get a song introduced, and not only did some of the performers use Foster's songs, but they subsequently stole them and had them published under their own names. Copyright laws for music were relatively lax in those days, and it was not unusual for the composer to arrange to have his songs published only to find that they had previously been published by someone else. Foster had this experience with "Oh! Susannah" and "Old Uncle Ned."

"Oh! Susannah" was written early in Stephen Foster's career, probably before he was twenty, and when he went to Cincinnati he got in touch with a publisher, W. C. Peters, to whom he either sold or gave away a number of his early pieces. Foster retained no royalty interest and although "Oh! Susannah" became a hit almost immediately, only Peters made money on it. The song was extremely "singable," and it became the theme song of the Forty-niners who sang it on their way to California in search of gold. It was included in every American minstrel performance for many years.

Because of his artistic success with "Oh! Susannah," Foster was offered contracts from two music publishers, one in Baltimore and one in New York. He gave up his bookkeeping job and married Jane McDowell, the daughter of a physician. During the first five or six years of his marriage, Stephen Foster wrote his best-known songs, including "Jeannie With the Light Brown Hair," "Old Folks at Home," "Massa's in de Cold Ground," "Old Dog Tray," "My Old Kentucky Home," "Gentle Annie," and "Come Where My Love Lies Dreaming." His publishers during this period were Firth, Pond, & Company and F. D. Benteen, and Stephen Foster earned a comfortable if not affluent living.

Stephen was not able, it seems, to apply what he had learned as a bookkeeper to his life as a composer, and he spent more during this period than he earned. By 1857 he had reached a financial crisis; he settled up with his publishers and sold songs outright for cash rather than royalties. The following year he was in financial trouble again and he made Firth, Pond, & Company his exclusive publisher and renegotiated a better contract. He lived with this arrangement for a while, but the songs published during the next year earned him royalties of only $700, and he again sold future rights to his publisher for a cash settlement and moved from Allegheny, Pennsylvania, where he had been living with his wife and young daughter, to New York City. Foster brought with him a song he had just written, "Old Black Joe," but it failed to live up to the expectations of his former hits and didn't earn the composer enough for him and his family to live comfortably in the city.

During the next four years Stephen Foster wrote over a hundred songs and none of them had the quality or success of his earlier songs. By this time Foster was using lyricists that he met in New York and was also drinking heavily. His salary contracts with his publisher ran out, and Foster began to sell to anyone who would publish his new songs. His wife could not stand the insecurity of life in New York with a husband who was seldom sober. She took her daughter and moved to Lewiston, Pennsylvania, where she made her home with her sister and found a job.

Stephen Foster evidently tried to reform and submitted to a variety of cures that his wife and family arranged for him, but he was unable to stop drinking. His family made an effort to get him to leave New York, but he wouldn't go. He was happier where he had many friends to drink with and who did not try to change his way of life.

Foster at last became ill, fell on a piece of crockery in his room at the North American Hotel and cut his throat. He was taken to Bellevue Hospital and died on January 13, 1864. He had written almost two hundred songs during his lifetime, twenty-five of which have become classic American folksongs and a half-dozen of which rank with the world's greatest ballads. There are many Stephen Foster songs that are not known today simply because they were not very good. Although Foster's early songs were written mainly for minstrel shows and are of a variety then called Ethiopian songs, Foster also wrote comic songs, Civil War songs, topical songs, and even some hymns.

Stephen Foster's earliest published song, "Open Thy Lattice, Love," was a tune he wrote for words written by George P. Morris that had been printed in the *New Mirror* on October 14, 1843. After he finished the composition a Philadelphia publisher, George Willig, published the song. Foster was then eighteen years old, and this early success was undoubtedly influential in his pursuing a songwriting career while he was also working as a bookkeeper.

"Old Folks at Home" was sold by Foster to E. P. Christy, the minstrel performer, for fifteen dollars. A condition of the sale was that Christy would be allowed to use his own name on the sheet music as composer. Foster did receive royalties for the song and later wrote to Christy for a release from his agreement. Christy apparently refused, and when the song became popular Foster was sorry that he had signed away his rights. It was not until the original copyright ran out that Stephen Foster was rightfully listed as the composer of one of his most admired songs.

A single American collector was responsible for the preservation of Stephen Foster relics. Josiah Kirby Lilly of Indianapolis recognized that Stephen Foster was America's greatest writer of folksongs, and he gathered a collection of Fosteriana for many years and housed it in a stone building on his property that was called Foster Hall. In 1937 Mr. Lilly gave the entire collection to the University of Pittsburgh, where a new building was erected to house it. The collection is now available to students and scholars.

Included in the collection is the little purse found on Foster when he was taken to Bellevue. It contained thirty-eight cents and a slip of paper on which was written "Dear friends and gentle hearts." The man who wrote some of America's greatest songs died with these possessions and the clothes on his back. The inventory of Stephen's possessions at his death included "coat, pants, vest, hat, shoes, overcoat."

First song written by Stephen Foster in 1844. His name appears on it with the wrong first initial.

Foster sold "Old Folks at Home" to E. P. Christy and allowed him to use his name. Published 1851.

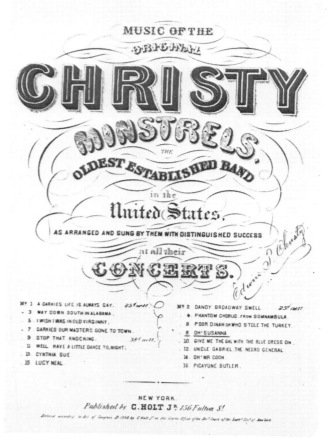

Foster's "Oh! Susannah" was a staple of Christy's Minstrels, as were many of the other songs written by composer. This was first song for which Foster received any money. Later, song became theme for the Forty-niners en route to California.

Sheet music for minstrel group includes Foster items, but his name does not appear on cover. Palmer lithograph, New York, 1848.

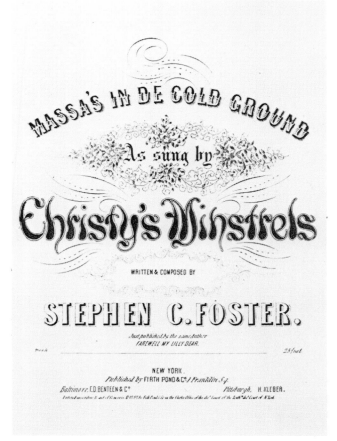

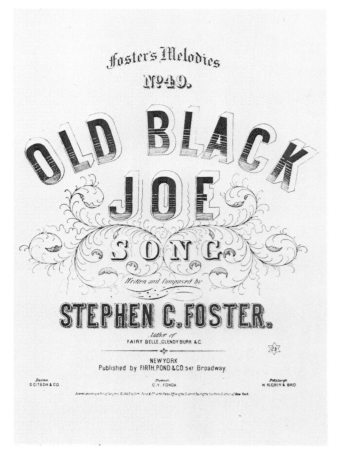

Well-known Foster song published in 1852. In two years it had sold almost seventy-five thousand copies.

This is one of few Foster Negro songs not written in dialect. The "Joe" of song was servant of Foster's wife's family before Fosters were married. "Joe" did not live to hear song, which was published in 1860.

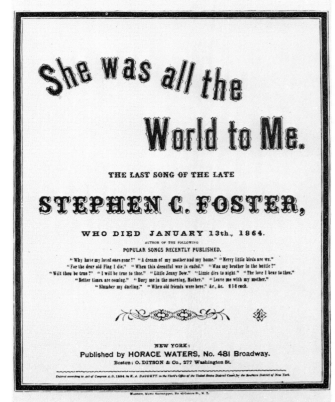

One of Foster's best-sellers, "Old Dog Tray," sold amost fifty thousand copies in first year it was published, 1853.

Foster died without a penny, but his songs continued to earn money for his publishers long after he was gone. His last song, published in 1864.

RAGTIME
AND SCOTT JOPLIN

In the nineteenth century a songwriter had little real protection for his music, and the most popular composers realized relatively little money for their published works. The music publishing business was disorganized in that there was no central place where music was published nor was sheet music sold in tremendous quantity, due to distribution problems and lack of a medium for national advertising. In addition, the only source of income for a composer from his music was the sale of the actual published sheets.

The one man most responsible for the American custom of "plugging" a new song until it became popular was Charles K. Harris whose "After the Ball" became the first all-time best-seller. Within twenty years after its publication the song had sold ten million copies, and after its first year of publication had earned its composer-publisher $25,000 a week. The song was the first million seller and it was marketed as such by Harris. It was translated into every foreign language, and every subsequent song that Harris wrote listed the composer as author of "After the Ball."

If the parlor piano was a woman's instrument in Foster's day, it had reached its peak of popularity by the time Harris was composing his songs right before the turn of the century. It was an instrument that was still mostly left to the ladies to play. The presence of a piano, especially a large bulky instrument with carving and dressed with shawls, draperies, vases, and family portraits in ornate frames, was a sure sign that an American family had "arrived." So had American business advertising and promotion as applied to the sheet music business.

It cannot be doubted that Harris truly believed in his tear-jerking songs. He cried himself whenever he sang the song that had made him a millionaire. Most of the popular ballads of the period were tearful, and the sadder the lyrics the better. Stephen Foster had had more reason to cry than did Charles

K. Harris. While Foster was always in need of money, Harris made his fortune early in his career. The answer was promotion. Furthermore, Harris had the good sense to become his own publisher and therefore made all the profits from his success rather than a small percentage. It probably mattered little that Harris had few great successes after "After the Ball." There are few people today who can hum, or would care to hum, the tunes to "Nobody Knows, Nobody Cares," or "Hello, Central, Give Me Heaven." However, all were promoted with the "Harris touch." Harris had had, after all, P. T. Barnum from whom to learn when it came to promotion and selling.

Around the same time that Charles K. Harris was living high on the proceeds from "After the Ball," a new sound was being heard in the land. *Musical Courier* of 1899 called this music "vulgar, filthy and suggestive" and said "the Pabulum of theatre and summer hotel orchestras is coon music." What had arrived on the scene was ragtime with its oddly syncopated polyrhythms and its cakewalk beat. Ragtime, *real* ragtime, lasted a very short time in America's musical history and during its first period of popularity was somewhat misunderstood. The ballad remained the mainstay of American popular music, but during the two decades that ran between the years 1897 to 1917 ragtime music was heard in the country, was adapted, copied, and crucified. It had some real believers and very many critics.

Ragtime music had its origins in the black musical rhythms of Africa and was first heard in the red-light districts of American midwestern cities. Pianists in brothels, saloons, and gambling houses played a style of music called "honkey-tonk," "jag-time," or "barrel-house." Even popular ballads could be "ragged" by the nomadic pianists who spent many long and underpaid hours playing piano with a style of syncopation that no one thought to write down as musical score.

There was one wandering rag musician who did not especially care for the only kind of life that seemed open to a black piano player at the end of the last century. Although his name today is synonymous with the best of ragtime music, Scott Joplin was one of many able composers and pianists who believed in the rag as a distinct and important form of American music. He wrote some ragtime operas and when one, *Treemonisha*, was performed before a Harlem audience, it was unsuccessful. The black audience was embarrassed by the story of how the American Negro had to throw off old voodoo superstitions if he was to progress in a modern (read *white*) world. Joplin, a musically educated black man, played the wrong tune for his own people.

Scott Joplin was aware of his talents, and his "Maple Leaf Rag" was a popular hit during his own lifetime. Contrary to present-day belief, Joplin was not obscure in his own time and had a strong feeling of self-worth. In addition to his operas he wrote many rags for piano and some earlier standard pop tunes. He came from Texarkana, Texas, and had had piano lessons as a child and learned advanced harmony in college. "Maple Leaf Rag," named after a honky-tonk club in which Joplin had worked in Sedalia, Missouri, was his first and greatest success. John Stark, a white man from St.

Louis, was Joplin's mentor and publisher, and Stark also published other ragtime greats such as James Scott and Joseph Lamb.

After Joplin's success with "Maple Leaf Rag," he composed more rags in a set form. He played some vaudeville but never went back to the honky-tonk business, which he hated. He thought of himself as "king of the ragtime composers" and felt that he wouldn't become a popular music hero during his lifetime, but that he would be rediscovered years after his death. He published a book of instructions for the performance of ragtime music, which he felt in its classic form should be a slow unrushed rhythm only to be performed by trained pianists.

Scott Joplin died in 1917. His influence and importance in the history of American popular music was not clearly understood until many years later when Rudi Blash wrote a book about ragtime music that was dedicated to Joplin's memory. *They All Played Ragtime*, published in 1950, placed ragtime and Joplin in their proper perspectives in the history of American music. It would take twenty more years, however, before the music of Scott Joplin would become as well-known to Americans as Charles K. Harris's "After the Ball."

The early rags were, of course, not exactly hummable, and the syncopation was difficult for any but the most highly trained classicists to play. Their publisher, John Stark, really believed in the music he published, and many of the titles given to the published rags were made up by the publisher rather than the composers. At no time since Joplin's death has true ragtime been really dead. It has always had its champions, but these have recently grown to a rather large and dedicated coterie of knowledgeable and dedicated musicians and musicologists. Joplin, not exactly obscure during his lifetime, is finally "king of the ragtime composers." His rags have been recorded on modern albums and tapes and are constantly being "discovered" by fans heavily into American nostalgia and others who truly understand and admire the ragtime style. In addition, the piano compositions written by Joplin in ragtime have recently been republished as a collection. These still require an accomplished pianist in order for them to be played the way they were intended. The beat as written by Joplin and his contemporaries would influence all popular American music that was written after it.

Although Scott Joplin is the best known of all the ragtime composers today, there were many other musicians, both black and white, who helped popularize the syncopated rhythms around the turn of the century. The first piano rag to be published was by a white composer, William Krell. His "Mississippi Rag" was published on January 25, 1897. Later that same year Thomas M. Turpin's "Harlem Rag" was published. James Sylvester Scott wrote thirty rags for piano solo. Among them were "Hilarity Rag," "Great Scott Rag," and his last, published in 1922, "Broadway Rag." A white composer, Ben R. Harney, was a pioneer of published ragtime music, although he wrote songs rather than piano pieces.

There were many others whose music predated the popular ragtime music of the twenties. Composer Eubie Blake's long lifetime spanned the era beginning before 1900 to the present when he has seen the old rags once again become popular. He wrote "Charleston Rag" in 1899 and in 1921, with Noble Sissle, wrote music and lyrics for the all-black revue, *Shuffle Along*. Written primarily for a black audience, the show played two weeks at the Howard Theater in Washington, D.C., a week in Philadelphia, and then moved to an auditorium on Sixty-third Street in New York, where it was an enormous success with audiences of both races and played five hundred and four performances before it closed. The Blake-Sissle hits from that show were "Love Will Find a Way," "Bandana Days," "He May Be Your Man but He Comes to See Me Sometime," and the song that became a standard, "I'm Just Wild About Harry." The success of *Shuffle Along* was the major cause for the first all-black revue to be performed on Broadway in 1928. Although Blake was not called upon to write for that show, he did write the basic score for *Blackbirds of 1930* which starred Ethel Waters. In more than three-quarters of a century of composing and performing Eubie Blake has seen popular music come full circle and oldtime rags have now taken their place in American musical history.

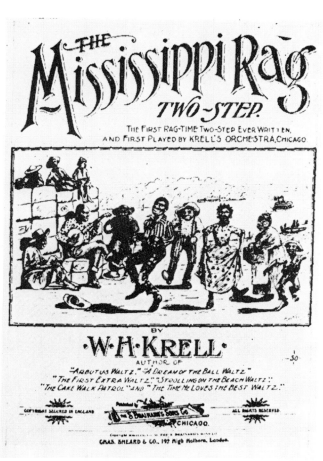

Earliest published classical rag, 1894.

Turpin's "Harlem Rag" was published in 1897.

Scott Joplin's earliest published rag was "Maple Leaf Rag."
This cover is from first publication by John Stark & Son in
Sedalia, Missouri, 1899.

Cover for 1901 edition of "Maple Leaf Rag."

"Original Rags" was written by Joplin, but Charles Daniels
helped him get it published and therefore got credit on cover,
1899.

When ragtime became popular every songwriter in the
business wrote syncopated songs and called them rags. This
one from 1912.

Even Chas. K. Harris got into the swing of ragtime and published this song in 1905.

One of the most famous of all popular rags is "Alexander's Ragtime Band," written by Irving Berlin in 1911.

Before "Alexander's Ragtime Band," Berlin wrote this less popular piece. The year was 1909.

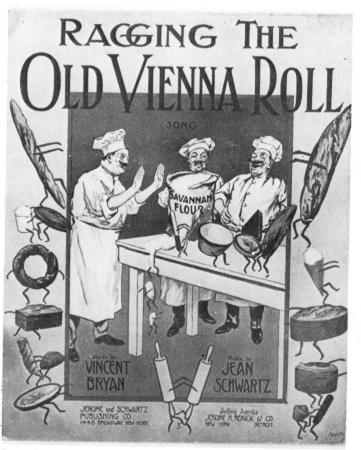

Everything got "ragged," including the "Old Vienna Roll," 1911.

A rag lullaby, 1912.

Even the sewing machine was used as a subject for a rag, 1912.

Coon songs were still an unfortunate fact of American music in 1914.

Sophie Tucker was famous in her early career as a coon-shouter. "The Darktown Strutters' Ball" was a ragtime classic popularized in 1917 by Miss Tucker and has been interpolated in several movies.

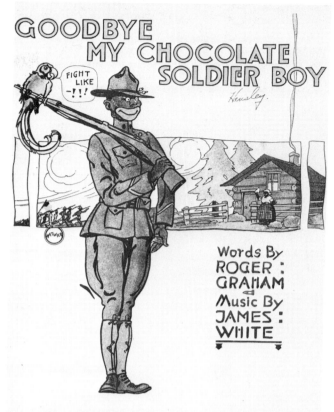

The way was short from rag to jazz. Sophie Tucker number from 1917.

World War I song, 1917.

Ragtime classic was first published as piano solo in 1914. Lyrics were added in 1919. This is original cover.

TIN PAN ALLEY

While Scott Joplin was writing down his syncopated rhythms that had no words and that originated in the bawdy houses of New Orleans and other cities, the vaudevillians were having a field day with a category of music that also was derivative of black music in America. We have already seen how the minstrels grew and developed a type of music of their own. As the minstrels became less and less important as a form of entertainment in America, the travelling vaudeville grew in importance. The "coon" song was the mainstay of all popular vaudeville, and not many stopped to think that the songs were vulgar and as racially biased as we now realize they were.

If America's songwriters wrote about what they knew, the one thing they were aware of in the decade between 1890 and 1900 was that the cities were being populated by great hordes of black people who left the South and rural areas to find work in metropolitan America. During that one decade more than six hundred coon songs were published, and although there might be few Americans who like to be reminded of this musical phenomenon today, the truth is that these were the most easily played and most often sung songs of that era. In addition, the mild-mannered southern black of Stephen Foster's day had become an urban threat and the popular songwriters did not go out of their way to ignore this. They formed their own stereotypes of the blacks they saw and cared little to understand them. The songs were often cruel and without any of the sensitivity of many of the earlier minstrel songs. By around 1910 the era of the coon song was almost over.

Although its origins were in the folk music of the South, the coon song was commercially popularized by vaudeville entertainer and pianist Ben Harney. Harney was a black man who passed for white, and he and other black performers such as Ernest Hogan and Irving Jones performed songs that, unlike the sentimental Foster songs, sustained the minstrel image of the lazy shuffling black man, the loose black woman, and the "primitive" relationship between the genders. Hogan's "All Coons Look Alike to Me" and Jones's "I'm Livin Easy Eatin' Pork Chops Greasy" not only kept "Old Zip Coon" alive but painted him as a worse individual than he had previously been. Harney claimed to be the inventor of ragtime, but his songs had little relationship to the musical compositions of Scott Joplin. However, these coon songs as popularized by Harney were undoubtedly the direct parents of popular rags, the type written by Irving Berlin and others.

Black performers who sang coon songs were one thing. Next came the white coon-shouters, which included among many May Irwin, Norah Bayes, and Sophie Tucker. They became known for their ability to belt songs into the last row of the balcony. In order to sustain her image, Sophie Tucker often included in her numbers a group of young black dancers who shuffled and cakewalked around her while she sang.

One of the reasons for the popularity of coon songs was that the cities were also being flooded around the turn of the century with many minorities from Europe, and they were excellent audiences for songs that insulted groups other than the ones they belonged to. In the same year that Charles K. Harris wrote "I've a Longing in My Heart for You, Louise" (a song that has become less than memorable since 1900 when it was written), Will Heelen and J. Fred Helf had a much more successful hit with "Every Race Has a Flag but the Coon." The following year Leo Friedman wrote "Coon! Coon! Coon!" It didn't take long for the immigrant songwriters to realize that they had found a good song form in their new homeland. In all fairness, not all coon songs were totally insulting. "Mighty Lak a Rose" was written the same year.

Israel Baline, who changed his name to Irving Berlin when he arrived in the United States, claimed he didn't know what ragtime was. Nevertheless, he wrote songs that were a popularized version of the syncopated rhythm. White rags became popular, beginning with "Alexander's Ragtime Band," which was written by Berlin in 1911. Any songs with a fast and peppy rhythm became known as "rag-time." The syncopation was adapted by many of the leading songwriters of the period, and every popular song subject was given a ragtime tune. "Ragtime Cowboy Joe" took the place of the coon songs, and even a song called "Ragtime Suffragette" was written. The rag that was being played was really a new type of music with roots in the disciplined music of Scott Joplin, but also out of the coon songs of the previous decade. Any syncopated musical piece could be called a rag.

If ragtime became the peppy music of the second decade of the century, blues became the ballad form. Again, we have the southern Negro to thank for what became a totally American form of popular song, and if we need to have a parent for every musical form, then W. C. Handy can easily be called the father of American blues. His "St. Louis Blues," an enormous hit in 1914, incorporated the rhythms of the two most popular dances of the era, the fox trot and the tango. During this decade social dancing had become extremely popular. Everyone danced to the great music of the era. Dance teachers across the country persisted in teaching the waltz and other "proper" dances, but America became tango-crazy as Irene and Vernon Castle became America's dancing darlings. Dance records began to sell in huge quantities.

Due to the new dance craze orchestras began to form in order to supply hotels and dance halls with live music for tea and evening dancing. Some of the earlier leaders of the big dance bands were Fred Waring, Vincent Lopez, Ben Bernie, and Ted Lewis. Paul Whiteman was a musical entrepreneur who organized several bands that supplied music for some of the larger hotels in the country. By 1922 Whiteman was head of a million dollar corporation with its own press agent and several orchestras.

It is interesting that many of the coon songs, blues songs, and dance numbers were written by men who had only recently become American citizens. By this time the music business was concentrated in one small area of New York City. The area around Twenty-eighth Street and Broadway became the home of American popular music, and its sounds could be heard coming from every open window of the buildings in the area as house writers pounded out tune after tune to keep up with the demand.

There are many conflicting legends of how this area became known as Tin Pan Alley. The one most popularly accepted is that the street sounded as though tin pans were constantly being clanged together. By the turn of the century the area and the business centered there were booming. The tangible product of Tin Pan Alley was sheet music, and each publisher had salesmen who plugged the songs in any way possible. Many years previous to this Stephen Foster had understood that in order to popularize a song it had to be performed. Charles K. Harris many years later also understood this. The music publishers of the early decades of this century used bribes to get popular performers to use their material, and later Payola record scandals certainly came as no shock to anyone who understands the history of song-plugging in America.

Just as each era provides its own literature and art, it also leaves its mark on the popular music of the time, and any songwriter who wasn't willing to move along with the times in the first decades of this century would find himself without a lucrative career. Even stuffy Charles K. Harris attempted to move from the nineteenth century by writing ragtime and coon songs. The ballad was still the mainstay of American pop, and during the first decade of this century some superb ballads were written. "Just A-Wearyin' for You" (words by Frank Stanton, music by Carrie Jacobs-Bond) was written in 1901; "Good Bye My Lady Love" was written by Joseph E. Howard in 1904 and was published by Harris; "My Gal Sal" was written by Paul Dresser in 1905; "Will You Love Me in December As You Do in May" had words by James J. Walker and music by Ernest R. Ball and was written in 1904.

By 1909 the country rang with the tunes of "Let Me Call You Sweetheart" and "Down by the Old Mill Stream." With all these "sing around the old piano" tunes the country was jazzin' it up, and the coonshouters were filling the vaudeville houses. Ever since the first coon song called "New Coon in

Town," the song that is said to have started it all back in 1887, there was strong competition for the ballad. Music was a booming business, and the buildings around Broadway that housed the major music publishers were partitioned off into small cubicles, each supplied with its battered and cigarette-scarred piano. The tunesmiths worked one to a cubicle, and the lyricists wandered from composer to composer supplying a word here and a phrase there, often making outlandish rhymes. The writers were mostly former newspapermen, and they became the folk poets of the era. Many of the immigrant songwriters had a poor command of the English language but were somehow able to capture the idiom of the period by reading and listening. Frequently, older tunes were "borrowed" to fit new words.

All real talent was welcome in this new and lucrative big-city industry. No matter that Irving Berlin couldn't read music and only composed in one key. The better-trained and more serious composer, George Gershwin, was also a familiar face on Tin Pan Alley. It was where the action was. The talented immigrants may have borrowed the style and sense of the black-oriented blues, but they understood the depression that lay behind them and adapted the blues form to their own words and sounds. They were bright and versatile and quickly grasped the American scene from which they drew their subject matter. By 1911 Irving Berlin was writing lines such as "Everybody's doing it. Doing what? Turkey trot." and had two ragtime hits, "Ragtime Violin" and "The Mysterious Rag."

The period from the turn of the century up until World War I was busy and prolific on Tin Pan Alley. A great many standards that are still enjoyed were written. We can go back to 1903 for "Ida! Sweet As Apple Cider!" which was later made popular by Eddie Cantor. *Babes in Toyland* was written that year by Victor Herbert, and it had great music, the best known of which is "March of the Toys." The same year Richard Gerhard and Harry Armstrong wrote "You're the Flower of My Heart, Sweet Adeline," and Richard Henry Buck and Theodore F. Morse wrote "Dear Old Girl."

A few of the hits of the next ten years were: "Meet Me in St. Louis, Louis" (words by Andrew B. Sterling, music by Kerry Mills); "The Yankee Doodle Boy" from *Little Johnny Jones* with words and music by George M. Cohan; "Dearie" by Clare Kummer; "In the Shade of the Old Apple Tree" (words by Harry H. Williams, music by Egbert Van Alstyne); "Mary's a Grand Old Name" from *Forty-five Minutes from Broadway* by George M. Cohan; "What You Goin' to Do When the Rent Comes 'Round—Rufus Rastus Johnson Brown" (words by Andrew B. Sterling, music by Harry Von Tilzer); "A Woman Is Only a Woman but a Good Cigar Is a Smoke" from *Miss Dolly Dollars* (words by Harry B. Smith, music by Victor Herbert); "Because You're You" from *The Red Mill* (words by Henry Blossom, music by Victor Herbert); "You're a Grand Old Flag" from *George Washington, Jr.* (words and music by George M. Cohan); "Cuddle Up a Little Closer" from *The Three Twins* (words by Otto Harbach, music by Karl Hoschna); "Take Me Out to the Ball Game" (words by Jack Norworth, music by Albert Von Tilzer); "By the Light of the Silvery Moon" (words by Edward Madden, music by Gus Edwards); "Heaven Will Protect the Working Girl" from *Tillie's Nightmare* (words by Edgar Smith, music by A. Baldwin Sloane); "I Wonder Who's Kissing Her Now" from *The Prince of Tonight* (words by Will M. Hough and Frank R. Adams and music by Joseph E. Howard and Harold Orlob); "Put on Your Old Gray Bonnet" (words by Stanley Murphy and music by Percy Wenrich). There were, of course, hundreds of other songs, many of which are still popular.

Since "After the Ball" the publishers looked for the hits that would make them millionaires. They gave the war some superb songs and would go into the roaring twenties with thriving businesses that would soon be threatened by the introduction of the new electronics.

One of most popular nonsense songs of its time (1869). Though published four years after Civil War it was favorite of black troops during conflict and was popularized in minstrels.

Typical coon song, 1894.

Although this song appears to have insulting title, its lyrics are about a girl to whom "all coons appear to look alike" because she only has eyes for a special young man. Ernest Hogan was black and was sorry later he had written the tune.

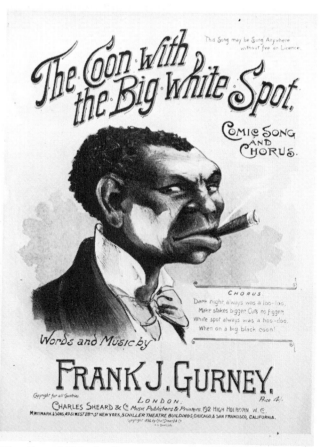

"The Coon With the Big White Spot" was a popular comic song in 1896. Cover lithograph is by H. G. Banks.

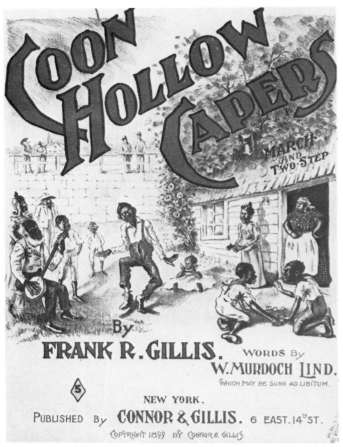

"Coon Hollow Capers," march and two step, 1899.

Comic Lew Dockstader introduced "Coon, Coon, Coon," in 1901.

One of few sheet music covers featuring black performers. They had a difficult time breaking into American theater and performed coon songs. Song published in 1901.

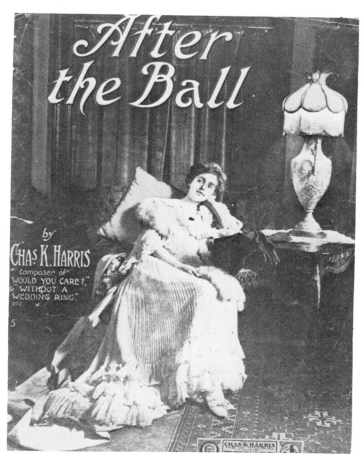

First pictorial cover for "After the Ball" has photographs of Charles K. Harris, author, and J. Aldrich Libbey, singer who interpolated song into show *A Trip to Chinatown*, 1892.

Later artistic cover for "After the Ball," song that made a fortune for Harris.

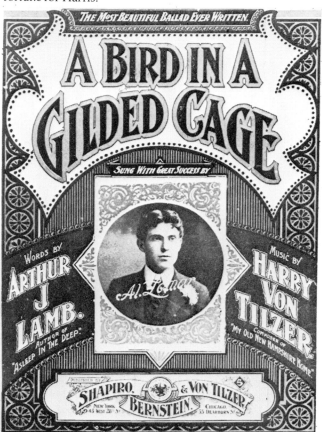

Charles K. Harris had a hit again with one of earliest "telephone" songs, 1901.

One of most successful ballads of 1900. Composer agreed to write music if Lamb made it clear that girl of the song was *not* millionaire's mistress but his wife. Von Tilzer tried out song first in brothel. He said he knew he had a hit when the girls cried at hearing it for first time.

Carrie Jacobs-Bond was one of country's few female songwriters at turn of the century. She couldn't get any of her songs published so she went into publishing business herself.

Charles K. Harris song, written 1903, was published by his own company and given a splendid Art Nouveau cover.

Music written by Kathleen A. Roberts in 1903.

Sentimental ballad popularized by barbershop quartets since 1903. Song was unsuccessful as "You're the Flower of My Heart, Sweet Rosalie" and no publisher would touch it until name was changed.

Popular song of 1906 became more popular when used in revue *Up and Down Broadway* in 1910. It was later used in many motion pictures.

Popular song, written in 1907.

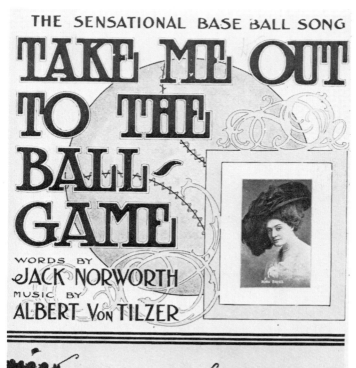

The unofficial baseball anthem, written in 1908. Writer didn't see a baseball game until twenty years later.

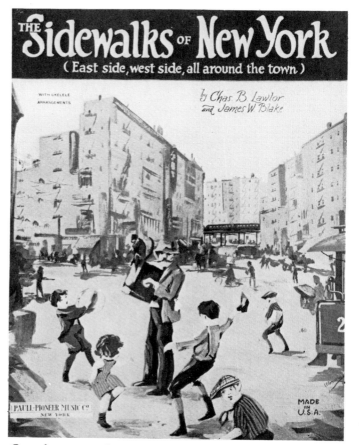

One of most popular songs to come out of New York, this was written in 1894 and has been published in many different editions.

Song giving the ultimate brush-off, 1908.

"The only comedy railroad song" has been popular since it was written in 1909.

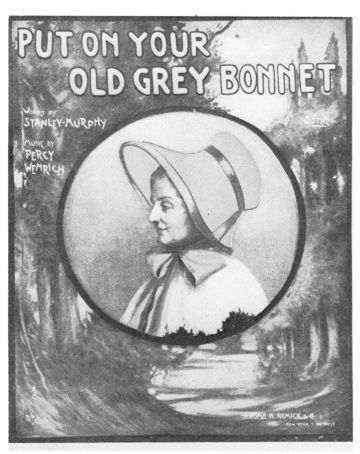

Hit song of 1909 sold over a million copies of sheet music.

One of country's most successful love ballads, first published in 1910.

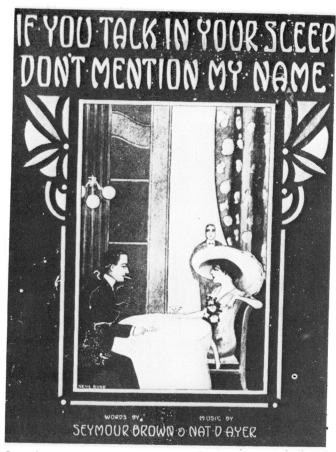

Song from 1911 is one of few from that period about adultery. Woman, at clandestine lunch with lover, tells him to be careful about mentioning her name if he talks in his sleep.

One of first "telephone" songs to use the phone on stage as a prop. Title was later used by Irving Berlin for love ballad. This version published in 1911.

Hit song of 1911 was plugged by Mose Gumble of Jerome H. Remick publishing house.

Irving Berlin song made effective use of babytalk and was popularized by Natalie Normandie in 1913.

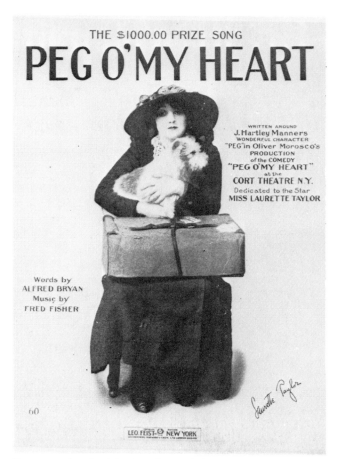

Song was inspired by hit show of the same title in 1912 and was dedicated to its star, Laurette Taylor, who is pictured on the cover.

Popular song of 1915.

One of Gus Kahn's earliest successes, published 1915.

One of many odes to Ireland and Mother, 1916.

Syrupy ballad of 1916 was popular with vaudeville fans.

Another song which sold over a million copies. First published as instrumental, words were added in 1916. It is now official state song of Missouri and was theme song for Harry Truman.

This song was popularized in 1920 by Paul Whiteman and his orchestra. The Victor recording was a million seller.

Cover for 1914 song to popular dances.

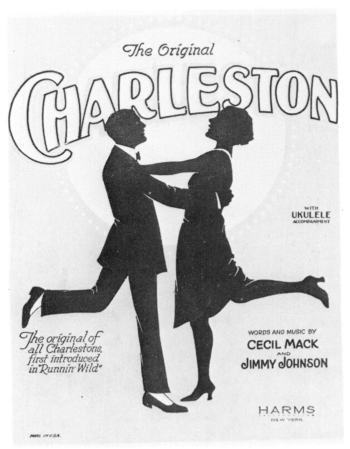

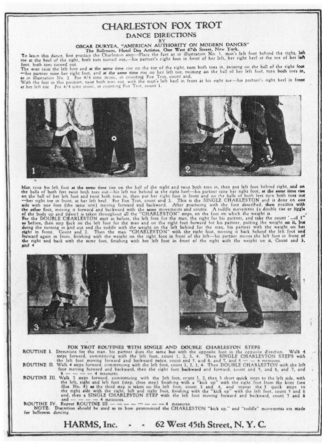

Cover for dance that swept country in 1920s. Back of cover gives directions for doing dance.

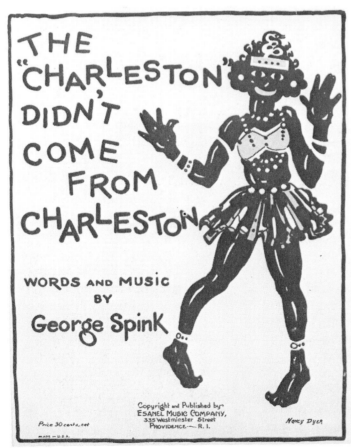

One of many "Charleston" songs published in the 1920s when dance was popular. Published in Providence, Rhode Island in 1926.

The turkey trot was a jazz age dance. Published in 1912.

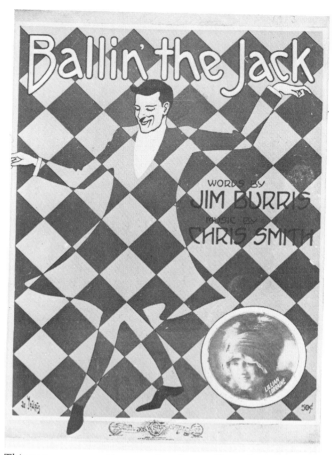

This song was a ragtime number that really makes no attempt to explain how the dance, a variation on the cakewalk, is done. Introduced in vaudeville in 1913.

Irene and Vernon Castle popularized the tango and many songs were written for it, this one in 1914.

"The Tango Flip," 1914.

A waltz popularized in vaudeville in 1920.

Song written for Eddie Cantor was inspired by newspaper cartoon in 1923. Vaudeville stars Olsen and Johnson used song to help their career and it is closely associated with them.

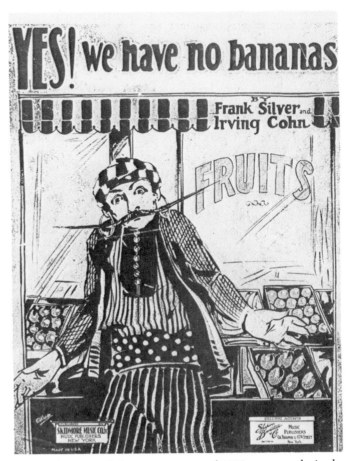

Extremely successful nonsense song of 1923 was popularized by Eddie Cantor.

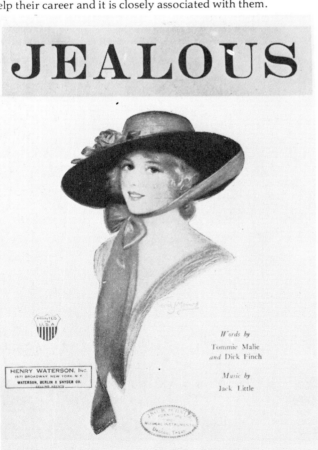

This 1924 song has cover design by Frederick S. Manning.

Irving Berlin's "All Alone" was written in 1924 while he was having a difficult love affair with Ellin Mackay, whom he subsequently married.

"Your lips tell me no, no" is the starting line for this hit song of the year 1924.

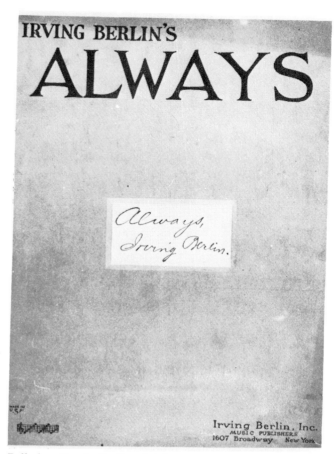

Ballad written by Berlin while he was courting Ellin Mackay in 1925. He gave his wife the rights to the song as a wedding gift.

Another hit song popularized by Eddie Cantor. Written in 1925.

Song, published in 1925, was popularized by Glen Gray and his Casa Loma Orchestra.

New York dialect song was great hit recording in 1925.

Popular hit based on Viennese song "Madonna," 1926. Buddy DeSylva wrote English lyrics.

Popular song of 1927 was used in 1929 movie, *It's a Great Life.*

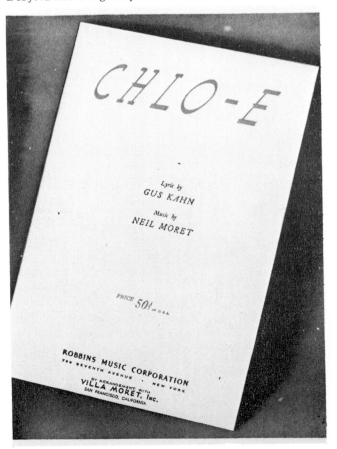

Song hit of 1927.

Hit song from musical *Great Day*, 1929.

Another Vincent Youmans hit, written in 1930.

"Body and Soul" was a hit in Europe before it became a success in the United States in 1930. It was originally written for Gertrude Lawrence and was later used in Max Gordon revue, *Three's a Crowd*.

One of many "moonlight" songs, this one written in 1930.

Depression song (1930) used in Billy Rose's revue *Crazy Quilt* in 1931.

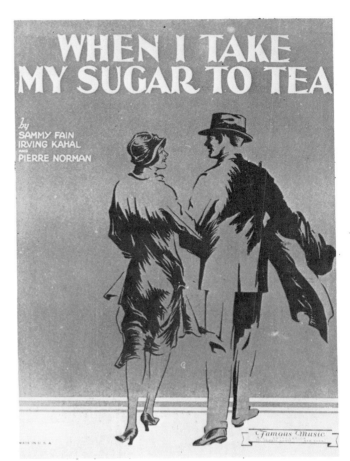

Song written in 1931 was interpolated in Marx Brothers movie *Monkey Business* later that year.

"Sophisticated Lady" was originally an instrumental written by Duke Ellington in 1933. When lyrics were added it became a hit.

Probably only popular song written about a French horn. Nonsense song was tremendous hit in 1935 and was later used by Danny Kaye in motion picture *The Five Pennies* (1959).

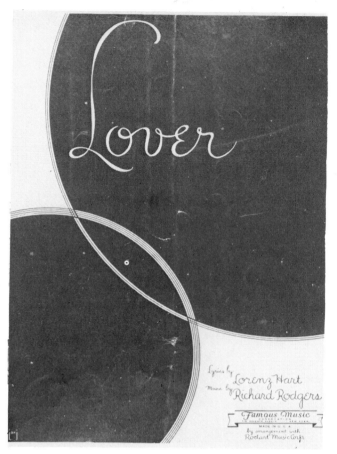

Sophisticated Art Deco cover for "Lover," Rodgers and Hart hit introduced in 1932 by Jeanette MacDonald in movie *Love Me Tonight.*

Song written in 1935 was used in musical *Spread it Abroad.*

Bluest of blues songs of the thirties has interesting cubistic cover. Tune was Hungarian, English words added in 1936.

Hit song of 1936.

"Organ Grinder's Swing," hit of 1936.

Song of 1939 was popularized by Kay Kayser and his orchestra. The record sold over a million copies.

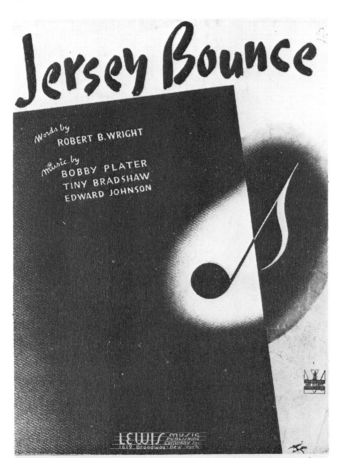

Originally an instrumental, this 1941 hit was popularized by Benny Goodman and his orchestra and Glenn Miller and his orchestra. Lyrics weren't added until 1946.

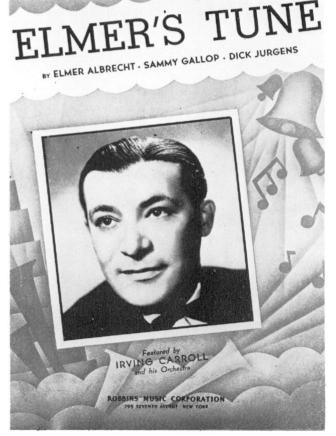

Song written in 1941 was popularized by Dick Jurgens and his orchestra.

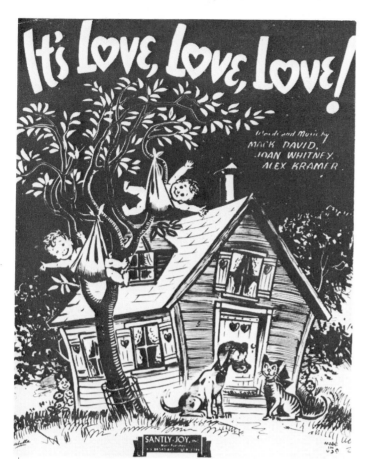

Song from 1943 popularized by Guy Lombardo and his Royal
Canadians on Decca record.

Song written by follower of yoga in 1946 was made popular
by Nat King Cole recording. It sold half a million records the
first month it was out and the song shot immediately to first
place on hit parade.

RECORDING
AND THE BIG BANDS

We have to remember that almost all popular music income was derived from the sale of sheet music in the first part of this century. There was no reason for the publishers of Tin Pan Alley to believe that this highly organized and widespread business would not go on forever. Even if the disk record had finally come into use in the early 1900s and replaced the cylinder record of the previous decade, the phonograph still didn't seem too much of a threat. After all, player pianos had only helped to popularize the best music of the period and spurred sheet music sales.

Early recordings were limited to the spoken word, solo singers (especially Enrico Caruso and other opera stars), and small orchestral groups. These records were available as early as 1913, but did not become commercially practical until the introduction of electronic recording methods in the 1920s. When radio was developed around the same time it would have taken a very stupid music publisher not to realize that something terrible was about to happen. Radio even caused a decline in the phonograph industry in the 1920s, and there was no longer any need to make one's own music on the parlor piano. The sound disturbed the family's favorite programs. One no longer had to rush to buy the latest popular song. It could be heard played and sung by professionals just by the turn of a dial. Any music you wanted to hear on demand could be purchased on one of those heavy black disks and played on the family Victrola. It would be more than two additional decades before the records could be played without any scratchy accompaniment, but the development of the long-playing record in 1948 finally began to put an end to what was already a dying business. Audible publishing was now the center of the pop music world. Who had to play the piano any more?

The country still needed new popular music and in larger quantities than before. Juke boxes blared all of the forties favorites, which were played so often that the soda fountain teenagers soon tired of them. Sheet music for all the popular tunes was still available, but the compulsion to own all of the latest songs was transferred from the printed music to the pressed sounds. Pianos stopped selling in quantity in the late twenties and thirties, and the same amount of money in the family budget went for the mahogany monster that blared recorded sounds throughout the house.

The music on the early records, apart from the classics, was that of the era performed by the popular stars. The old coon songs were great favorites and "Mr. Gallagher and Mr. Sheehan," "Cohen on the Telephone," and other dialect songs of the period were purchased in quantity. The recording quality was scratchy on the early records, but this made no difference if one could wind up the machine and hear Sophie Tucker any old time.

By 1914 the social dance craze had come in, and home music was needed for that. Regardless of what the theater managers, threatened by a falling off of business, said, the phonograph could take the place of live entertainment. You no longer had to go out of the house to hear a good sentimental ballad sung by a famous recording star.

Related industries often are helpful to one another and radio eventually helped the recording and phonograph business. Both would hurt the sheet music publishing industry so badly that it would never make a comeback. Collectors who specialize in sheet music of the first thirty years of this century will find the covers of many of the popular songs of the thirties have photographs of the recording stars who introduced many of the songs. In addition there are many stars on sheet music covers of the thirties and forties who made their fortunes in radio. Songwriters kept feeding the stars and the new media material throughout the waning years of music publishing, but it wasn't until the music publishers, composers, and lyricists banded together to protect their properties that they would earn their due from the radio and phonograph promoters.

An important aspect of the phonograph was it's adaptability to the sounds of an orchestra, and with the development of jazz and swing the big bands that were formed became well known through their recordings. In the thirties and forties, especially, everyone became familiar with all of the great bands that were formed, and a single hit song would be recorded by several different orchestras. The dance craze continued throughout this period, and this required more and more new recordings. The big bands survived until World War II, and the sheet music with photographs of the leaders of bands that were most famous are now an important documentation of the "swing" period of American popular music. The Dorseys, Sammy Kaye, Cab Calloway, Duke Ellington, Benny Goodman, Guy Lombardo, and many others were all responsible for the thousands of hit orchestral arrangements of popular tunes during the thirties and forties. They all established individual orchestral sounds that were as easy to distinguish to the teenagers of the forties as the various rock groups are to the teenagers of today.

Music written to the machine that eventually ruined the music publishing business. No one dreamed in 1878 that the phonograph would be anything more than a novelty or helpful office aid.

Sousa was leader of one of the earliest big bands to be recorded and broadcast over radio.

Many college songs were written around 1930. This one was a great success. Rudy Vallee wrote the music.

One of Duke Ellington's first popular hits, this song was first published under title "Dreamy Blues."

SMOKE RINGS

MUSIC BY
H. EUGENE GIFFORD

LYRIC BY
NED WASHINGTON

Lawrence
MUSIC PUBLISHERS INC.

Good Night, Little Girl Of My Dreams

by
CHARLIE TOBIAS
and
JOE BURKE

B. A. ROLFE
and his
TERRAPLANE
ORCHESTRA

JOE MORRIS MUSIC CO.
MUSIC PUBLISHERS
1619 BROADWAY
NEW YORK CITY

Music written and published in 1932 became theme song of Glen Gray and his Casa Loma Orchestra.

Some of the big bands did not make it into the bigtime in recording and radio. This is a song from 1933, featured by B. A. Rolfe and his Teraplace Orchestra.

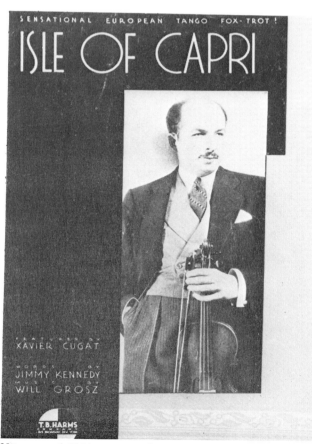

SENSATIONAL EUROPEAN TANGO FOX-TROT!

ISLE OF CAPRI

XAVIER CUGAT

WORDS BY
JIMMY KENNEDY

MUSIC BY
WILL GROSZ

T.B. HARMS

RAIN

Words by
BILLY HILL
Music by
PETER DE ROSE

PHIL HARRIS

Shapiro
Bernstein
& Co.
MUSIC PUBLISHERS
Capitol Theatre Building
Broadway & 51st Street
New York

Barbelle

Hit song of 1934 was popularized by Xavier Cugat. It sold over a million copies of sheet music and three million records.

Phil Harris on cover of 1934 song.

Hit from 1936 as featured by George Olsen and his orchestra.

Song written in 1916 was revived by Blue Barron and his orchestra in 1937 and popularized again in 1940 by Bing Crosby.

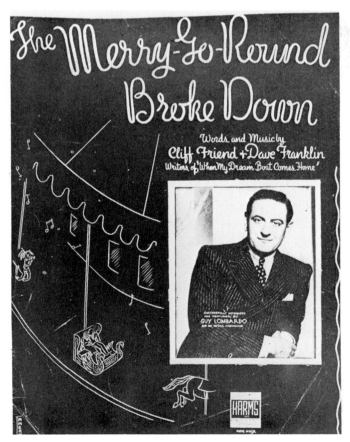

Song from 1937 is now mostly forgotten but it was enormous hit when first written. It was featured by Guy Lombardo and his Royal Canadians.

Hit of 1938 was featured by Lawrence Welk.

This song was introduced in musical *Right This Way* but was not a hit until Freddy Martin and his orchestra recorded it in 1943 and it became one of hit ballads of World War II.

Now mostly forgotten, this song was written in 1938 and was a big recording hit.

Frankie Carle, Glen Gray, and Glenn Miller all had hit recordings with this 1939 favorite.

Recording of this pop song by Benny Goodman, with vocal by Martha Tilton and trumpet solo by Ziggy Elman was extremely successful in 1939.

Cab Calloway and his Cotton Club Orchestra had a hit with "The Jumpin' Jive" in 1939.

Popular Spanish song was given English lyrics and was an Artie Shaw million-record seller in 1940.

UNTIL TOMORROW
by SAMMY KAYE

Sammy Kaye

REPUBLIC MUSIC CORP.
730 - 5th AVENUE NEW YORK

Sammy Kaye wrote and recorded "Until Tomorrow" in 1940.

Leading song hit of 1941. Most popular record of it was made by Mills Brothers.

Jimmy Dorsey and 1941 song.

Horace Heidt and his Musical Knights, 1941.

Tommy Dorsey and favorite song of 1942.

Kay Kayser and hit of 1942.

Les Brown and the Duke Blue Devils on 1940 song hit with tune adapted from 1844 song "Lubly Fan."

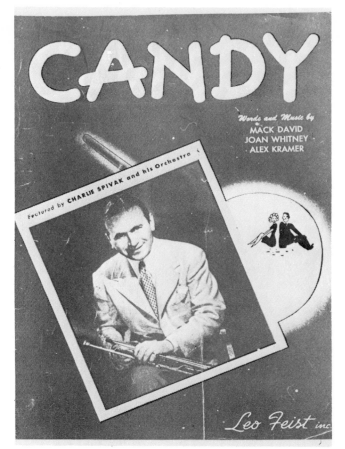

Although Charlie Spivack is featured on this cover of "Candy" it was made popular by recordings by Johnny Mercer, Jo Stafford, and the Pied Pipers in 1944.

Song that was Harry James's hit record in 1944.

Song that was Gene Krupa's hit recording in 1944.

Hit of 1945 was title song for Gene Autry movie the following year.

This song was not a hit, but the novelty cover makes it desirable to sheet music collectors. Recorded in the 1940s by Freddy Martin and his orchestra.

THE STARS
AND SONGS OF RADIO

Remember Radio? Not the radio of disk jockeys, rock, and news, but real Radio with live programs and stars and great songs you could hum afterward. Radio, and popular music's history along with it, has had a peculiar history in America. If David Sarnoff had the miraculous idea to make radio a household utility he certainly succeeded, and after World War I there was, as he had promised, music in almost every American home in the form of a "radio music box." Music became the staple of radio from the start because it used up time most easily. Station KDKA Pittsburgh was the first radio station on the air, and two years later there were six hundred stations using up the air waves. This number was cut back during the Depression years, but by 1940 there were eight hundred AM stations operating. By 1949 there were eighty million radio receivers in the United States and twelve million of these were in automobiles.

Early radio had a strong effect on the types of songs that were written. The radio was, at first, a superb medium for song-plugging and the music was provided free of charge. It soon became obvious to the writers and publishers that they were being used unfairly when programs began to be sponsored and the stations were making all the money. The sales of sheet music dropped gradually as radio replaced the piano as home entertainment. You didn't have to buy the popular songs and learn how to play them. All you had to do was to turn the dial and you could hear your favorite song sung by one of many popular performers.

Special songs were written for performances on radio, and the medium made its own stars, who became even better known as the recording industry developed. Orchestra music was especially suited to radio, and the big bands could be broadcast from any place in the country. Vincent Lopez was the first bandleader to broadcast from his regular night spot, the Pennsylvania Grill in New York. Business picked up considerably as the nightclub received publicity from the radio show, and many other bands followed suit. By 1930 75 percent of all radio time was taken up by dance music.

For vocalists radio was a bonanza. A voice that was easily recognized had a better chance of audience identification, and radio made stars of performers whose voices seemed best suited to the medium. Rudy Vallee, Kate Smith (billed as the Songbird of the South), Ben Bernie, Bing Crosby, and many others were heard constantly over the airwaves. Radio exposure helped record sales and made successes of singing groups such as the Andrews Sisters and others who copied the style.

Perhaps the most popular of all early radio stars was Rudy Vallee who opened every program with a "Hi Ho, Everybody" in a mellifluous voice that became familiar to the entire nation. Vallee's Connecticut Yankees broadcast from the Heigh Ho Club on East Fifty-third Street in New York, and the musician announced his own musical selections. He was the first of many American "crooners." In a search for more and more musical material old songs were trotted out and among these was "The Stein Song," which became one of Vallee's biggest hits.

Vallee, billed as the Vagabond Lover, had his female counterpart in that perennial favorite, Kate Smith. Both took themselves very seriously and both had the talent and capacity to make hits out of songs they plugged on the radio microphones. Kate Smith, now known among younger audiences for her hefty rendition of Irving Berlin's "God Bless America," had an immense following of adoring fans who melted every time she belted "When the Moon Comes over the Mountain," her theme song. Both stars were apple-pie Americans who could hardly be considered sex symbols. They always pleased and never offended. From their radio exposure their records sold in huge quantity.

Radio, by the thirties, was big business. The station owners made money from sponsors, and the stars were well paid. The songwriters who provided most of the material that filled the air waves were the orphans of the industry that balked at paying for what they considered "free" advertising. Writers and publishers should, according to the broadcasters, be happy to have their songs "plugged" for nothing on the programs. Fortunately, the songwriters had their own association, ASCAP (The American Society of Composers, Authors, and Publishers), which felt differently. They were an elite group with members such as Victor Herbert, Irving Berlin, George Gershwin, Jerome Kern, Cole Porter, and many other successful writers. By 1939 ASCAP had tried in vain to establish an arrangement suitable to its members and to the National Association of Broadcasters (NAB) whereby certain royalties would be paid on every song played or sung on radio. No agreement between the two groups could be found, and radio decided it could do without the great musical talent of America's foremost songwriters. ASCAP had won its fight in Congress, but the broadcasters decided to go back to music that was out of copyright, anything published before 1884, and to do without the work of the established contemporary composers.

In those days ASCAP was a rather exclusive club, composed only of those music writers who had proved their talent. Writers of "lesser" hillbilly and cowboy songs and the nonprofessional would-be songwriters were happy to have their songs played on the air, and the broadcasters, in addition to using out-of-copyright music, turned to the amateur for material. For them they organized a new society, Broadcast Music Incorporated, which was intended to organize the lesser writers for the glory of radio and possibly to fake out the ASCAP members. BMI was organized on October 14, 1939. The broadcasters then waited to find out what rates ASCAP would set on its music. The war continued and in 1941, when ASCAP's rates were announced and turned out to be a 100 percent increase over what they had previously been, the broadcasters refused to pay, and for almost an entire year the music of the best contemporary American composers was cut off the air.

The broadcasters went back to our old friend, Stephen Foster, and his songs were played *ad nauseam* on radio all over the country. There were at least four hundred arrangements of "Jeannie with the Light Brown Hair" and everyone got sick of "Camptown Races" as swung by Ray Noble and his orchestra. Nineteenth-century ballads were pulled out of the closet and dusted off to be arranged to the new swing sound. Most of the new BMI music was terrible, although some hits did come out of this struggle. There was no public outcry, however, and ASCAP finally came to terms with the broadcasters.

One result of the ASCAP-BMI war was that almost everyone who grew up in the forties developed a strong disliking for all of Stephen Foster's music. Another was that the opportunity for the playing of hillbilly, cowboy, and other folk music was greater than it might have been, and it is probable that the radio exposure of this kind of music opened the door to the later rock and roll and country western styles.

"Radio" song, 1924.

Performers became associated with products sponsored on radio. Song used to promote brand of shoes in 1920.

"Carolina Moon," written in 1928, became radio theme song of singer Morton Downey.

Song was popularized on radio by Rudy Vallee after its publication in 1929.

Vallee also popularized this 1929 hit on his radio program.

Vallee introduced this old college song on his radio program in 1930 and it became a hit.

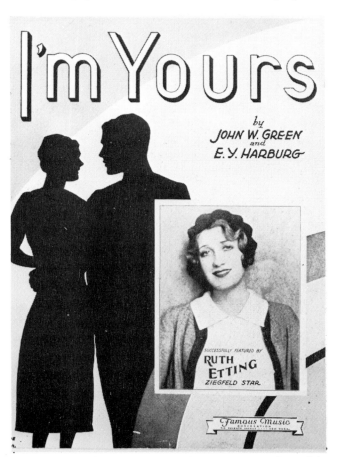

This Green and Harburg song of 1930 was popularized by Ruth Etting.

Kate Smith, "Songbird of the South," was star of radio when this music was published in 1932.

The mellifluous voice of Ben Bernie was easily recognizable on radio in 1932.

Bing Crosby in 1932.

Connie Boswell introduced this 1933 song.

Cover of famous Johnny Mercer-Hoagy Carmichael standard, written in 1933, has photo of hillbilly radio group that includes Judy Canova, who later became film star on her own.

Hit of 1934 became standard.

Theme song of Hildegarde was written by her manager in 1935. Nat King Cole made hit record of it.

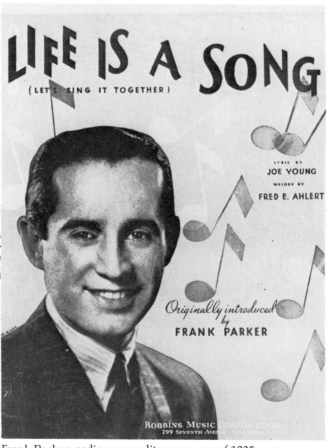

Hit song of 1935 was played over radio often.

Frank Parker, radio personality, on cover of 1935 song.

Sophie Tucker on cover of 1936 song.

Andrews Sisters on cover of one of their biggest hits in 1939.

"Mister Meadowlark" was recorded by Johnny Mercer, who also wrote the lyrics, and Bing Crosby in 1940.

Crosby hit of 1943.

Recording and radio star, Perry Como, on 1925 song resurrected in the 1940s.

Hit song of 1943 was also recorded successfully by the Andrews Sisters.

Frank Sinatra, "the Voice That Is Thrilling Millions," on cover of hit song of 1943.

Andrews Sisters swung this oldie (1917) to success in the early 1940s.

Song of 1944 was sung by Marion Hutton in Abbott and Costello film *In Society*.

Ginny Simms, star of Philip Morris radio program, 1944.

Song inspired by popular radio comedy program in 1944. It was really written by Abe Burrows and Frank Loesser.

Song originally introduced over the radio by Phil Brito in 1945.

Kate Smith did her bit during World War II by introducing many wartime songs. "Don't Worry Mom," 1944.

Wartime song popularized by Sinatra in 1945.

Cover has photos of stars from radio program "Chesterfield Supper Club," 1945.

Sheet music cover with many famous radio and recording stars of 1946.

IT'S A GOOD DAY

By PEGGY LEE and DAVE BARBOUR

Song written by Peggy Lee and Dave Barbour was recorded by Peggy Lee in 1946.

Patti Page was also a well-known radio and recording star in 1948.

Carolyn Leigh-Cy Coleman hit of 1958 has cover showing Tony Bennett at the mike.

Drawing of Peggy Lee on Barbara Fried-Milton Schafer sheet music published in 1970.

SONGS OF THE
AMERICAN MUSICAL THEATER

Historians of the American musical theater collect songs from the shows of this century that represent the development of the musical theater in the United States. In addition to artistic merit many of the sheet music covers carry a wealth of information on them. In what is usually an artistic arrangement of pictures and text the sheet music cover tells us who wrote the lyrics and music of each show, who wrote the book, who produced and directed the show, and sometimes what stars were featured. Only the date is inside the cover in the copyright notice. Often the covers for songs from American musical theater productions are handsomely designed. The productions were often so costly that the additional expense of an artistic cover was not considered prohibitive. Frequently, in the past, the cover was the same design used for advertising posters for a show.

The musical play as we know it in this century had its beginnings in several earlier forms of theater. Plays with music had been produced all through the nineteenth century, and opera as well as operettas had been produced in this country for a long time. The comic operas of Gilbert and Sullivan, Strauss, and Offenbach were probably the strongest and most direct influence on the development of American musical theater. In the 1880s and 1890s European operettas and comic operas dominated the American stage. In 1878 Gilbert and Sullivan's comic opera, *Pinafore*, opened at the Boston Museum, and it was an instant triumph. In a single season ninety different companies performed *Pinafore* throughout the country, and it was one of the first musical theater performances in this country that was thought to be proper for women and children to attend.

In the early 1800s satire and burlesque were the usual forms of musical production. This is not the burlesque of later years, but its emphasis was on parody and caricature. This form and the minstrels were also influential on the later development of American musical theater. Elements from ballad, opera, minstrels, and burlesque as well as vaudeville were all absorbed by twentieth-century writers of American musicals. The pantomime extravaganza also contributed to the twentieth-century musical play form.

Besides opening up the theater as a wholesome area of entertainment for women and children, the Gilbert and Sullivan play *Pinafore* also encouraged American writers to attempt to emulate its success. As other Gilbert and Sullivan operettas were produced in this country there were many obvious attempts to either parody or copy the successful formula of the British librettist and composer. The operettas of Victor Herbert, Rudolph Friml, and Sigmund Romberg were successful productions of the earlier part of this century and all had roots in the European operetta form. All of the works of these men contained extravagant production numbers, song, dance, comedy, and some burlesque.

The European personality of American operettas began to disappear with the productions of George M. Cohan, who, in the early part of this century, wrote musicals like *George Washington, Jr., Little Johnny Jones,* and *Forty-five Minutes from Broadway,* all of which had a distinctly American flavor. Cohan's productions were energetic, racy, and spirited, and they had a distinct influence on shows such as A. Baldwin Sloane's *The Summer Widowers* (1905) and *Hen Pecks* (1911). Irving Berlin's *Watch Your Step* also appears to have been influenced by Cohan.

At the same time that American musical comedy was coming into existence another form of theatrical production was evolving on the American stage. This was the musical revue, which was an obvious outgrowth of the earlier minstrel and vaudeville shows. Thrown in were elements of the extravaganza (100-beautiful girls-100) and the comedy acts of burlesque. George W. Lederer is thought to be the father of the musical revue. His *Passing Show,* which opened at the Casino Theater in New York in 1894, was so successful that similar revues opened almost immediately. Florenz Ziegfeld opened his first *Follies* in 1907; J. J. Shubert his *Passing Show* in 1912; and George White's first *Scandals* opened in 1919. By 1921 Irving Berlin wrote the first of his *Music Box Revues.* The early revues were handsomely produced with extravagant sets and costumes, and some of our best popular songs were written for them. "Everybody on stage for the big production number" was heard in theaters all over New York as each producer tried to outdo the others in skits, songs, dances, blackouts, and especially, the extravaganza, which included huge choruses and elaborate costumes and sets.

There is a wealth of music from the revues and musical comedy productions of the 1920s and 1930s. Songs by Jerome Kern, Cole Porter, Lorenz Hart and Richard Rodgers, Otto Hauerbach (later changed to Harbach when he got sick of the misspellings), Irving Berlin, George Gershwin, and many others contributed to a musical literature that is distinctly American. If any single composer is responsible for the American musical comedy form it is Jerome Kern. His production of *Show Boat* in 1927 was a turning point in that his characters were three-dimensional and the plot, based on the Edna Ferber novel, was much more complex than books for previous American shows.

The history of the American musical theater of the thirties reflected the economic problems that beset the country in those years. There were fewer extravagant musicals produced, but the quality of the music, lyrics, and books continued to improve. *Of Thee I Sing*, the satirical musical comedy of George Kaufman, the Gershwins, and Morrie Ryskind won a Pulitzer prize, and in 1935 George Gershwin's *Porgy and Bess* was produced.

The forties had its own classic musical plays and one of the first of the decade was Rodgers and Hart's *Pal Joey*, based on short stories by John O'Hara. When Rodgers and Hammerstein teamed up they wrote the historically significant and original shows *Oklahoma, Carousel, The King and I*, and *South Pacific*. American musical theater reached a high point with these classic productions.

Cole Porter's *Kiss Me Kate*, Harold Arlen's music for *Bloomer Girl* and *St. Louis Woman*, Frank Loesser's *Guys and Dolls* (based on Damon Runyon's short stories), and Irving Berlin's rich score for *Annie Get Your Gun* all came out of the forties and fifties. One of the highest points in the American musical theater was the 1956 production of *My Fair Lady* by Alan Jay Lerner and Frederick Loewe. Just a year later New York had its opening of Leonard Bernstein's *West Side Story*. There are, of course, many other superb and significant shows from the thirty years or so that American musical comedy flourished. Many of them are represented on song sheets illustrated in this chapter.

More recently the New York stage has had the most successful of all musical comedies—*Fiddler on the Roof* with book by Joseph Stein (based on stories by Sholem Aleichem), lyrics by Sheldon Harnick, and music by Jerry Bock. The show opened in 1964 and out-of-town reviews said it was "no blockbuster." Its New York reviews, however, were raves, and it is the longest-running Broadway musical play in America's history. In addition, it has been produced in countries all over the world including Czechoslovakia, Iceland, and Japan.

Two shows that were outstanding in the 1970 season were *Applause* (book by Betty Comden and Adolph Green, based on the motion picture *All About Eve*, and music by Charles Strouse and lyrics by Lee Adams) and *Company* (book by George Furth, lyrics and music by Stephen Sondheim). The first is a show about show business and the second a social commentary on marriage.

Most recently, the New York theater seems to have caught the nostalgia bug and the musical comedy of 1925, *No, No, Nanette* (book by Otto Harbach, lyrics by Otto Harbach and Irving Caesar, music by Vincent Youmans) was again a success. Two standards from the show, "I Want to Be Happy" and "Tea for Two" were dusted off and heard again. Another nostalgia item was *Irene* (book by James Montgomery, lyrics by Joseph McCarthy, music by Harry Tierney), a 1919 musical that made stage history in its time by being the longest-running Broadway production up until that time. "Alice Blue Gown" was the outstanding hit song of that show. Interestingly, the show was not made into a motion picture until 1940.

The New York musical theater has been the source of thousands of hit songs, many of which were used once again in films based on the original live productions. Since the musical theater's rise and development coincides with the development of the recording industry, there are many collectors who prefer to collect original cast recordings of the show tunes. Frequently, the record jackets and albums have the same designs as the sheet music that was published with each opening. However, the sheet music, no matter how inaudible, is a reminder of the great musical heritage given us by the talented men and women who have written the best American popular music of this century.

Victor Herber hit show of 1903.

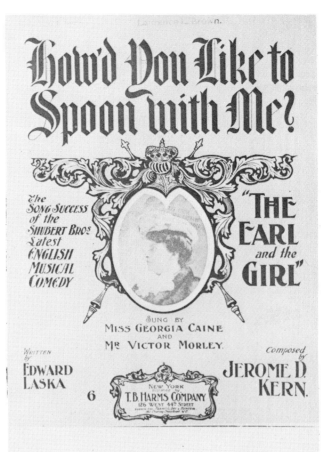

Jerome Kern wrote music for this Shubert show in 1905.

Lew Fields's production of 1905.

Buster Brown was hit show of 1906.

Sheet music from George M. Cohan's second success on Broadway, produced in 1906.

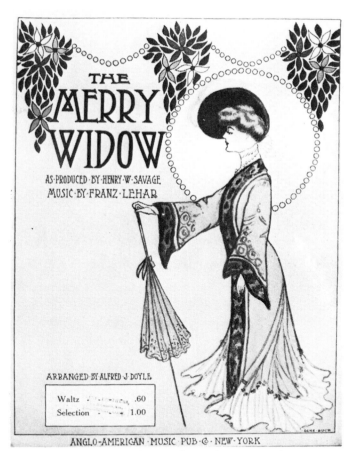

Operettas were extremely popular at beginning of century. Franz Lehar hit of 1907.

Song, written by Nora Bayes and Jack Norworth, became theme song for Miss Bayes but sheet music shows another Ziegfeld star, Ruth Etting, in 1908. This was the second *Ziegfeld Follies*.

Song from musical production of 1909.

Lo, a less-than-successful musical comedy of 1909, had book and lyrics by O. Henry and Franklin P. Adams.

Cover from music of *The Chocolate Soldier*, Oscar Strauss, 1909.

Elsie Janis on cover from song featured in 1911 stage production.

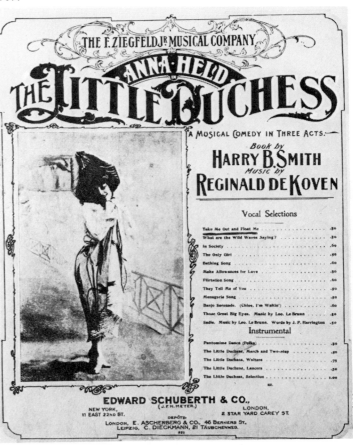

Song, "Take Me Out and Float Me," from Ziegfeld musical starring Anna Held in 1910.

Cover of song from vaudeville musical in 1912.

Not the well-known "Ramona," but a song written for musical *Roly-Poly* in 1913.

Eddie Cantor in one of his first appearances for Ziegfeld, around 1917.

Hit song from musical *Irene*, which was great success in 1919. It had longest run of any musical up to that time.

Two of many hit songs from musical extravaganza, *Sinbad*, 1918. "Swannee," popularized by Jolson, sold over two million records and a million copies of sheet music and was Gershwin's first hit.

Song from show produced in 1920.

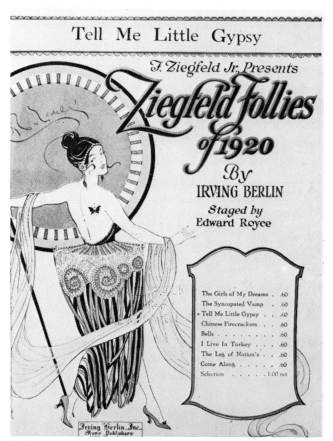

Follies of 1920 starred, among others, Mary Eaton, W. C. Fields, and Fanny Brice.

Fanny Brice on cover of song she made famous in 1920 revue.

"Mon Homme" was French sensation in 1920.

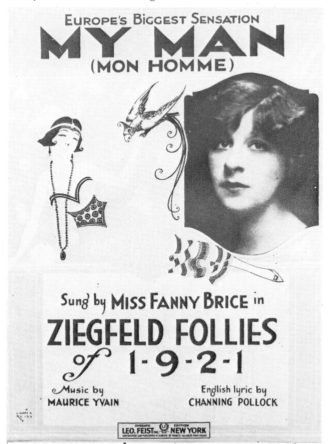

With English lyrics "My Man" was included in the *Ziegfeld Follies of 1921,* and Fanny Brice had another hit.

Eddie Cantor performing "mammy" song in 1921 production.

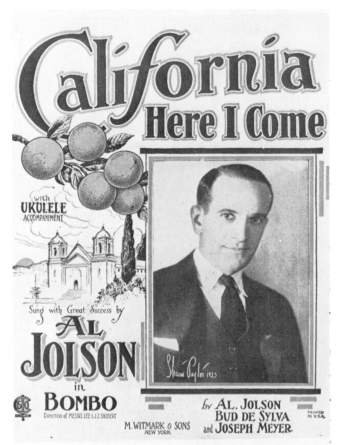

Al Jolson in two of the hit songs from *Bombo*, 1921.

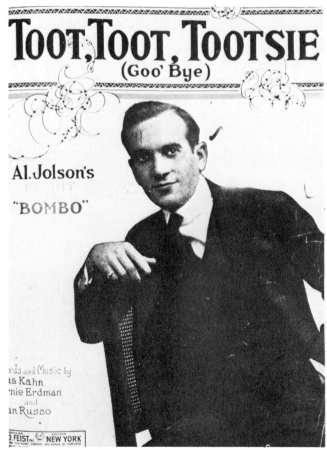

This song from *Bombo*, 1921, became hit of Jolson's film *The Jazz Singer*, 1928.

Hit song from musical comedy success *Shuffle Along*, 1921.

Nora Bayes, star of the twenties, as she appeared in musical revue.

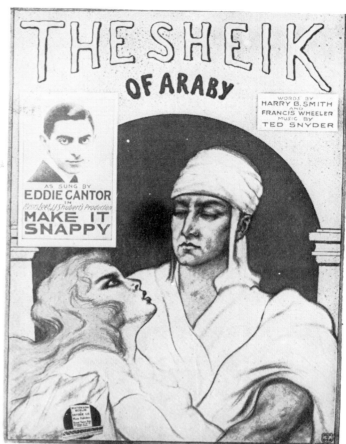

Song introduced by Eddie Cantor in Shubert production of 1921.

Hit of *Ziegfeld Follies of 1922* was also early recording sensation.

Covers for songs from *Music Box Revue* were all similar in design. Berlin's revues ran from 1921 to 1924.

George M. Cohan production of 1922.

Musical comedy that derived title from the Stone family that starred in it.

Ziegfeld production that ran almost five hundred performances starred Eddie Cantor in 1923. Show also featured Irving Berlin number, "Dinah."

Nora Bayes as she appeared in musical in 1923.

Song introduced in 1925 musical that has recently been revived.

French sheet music for "Tea For Two," 1924.

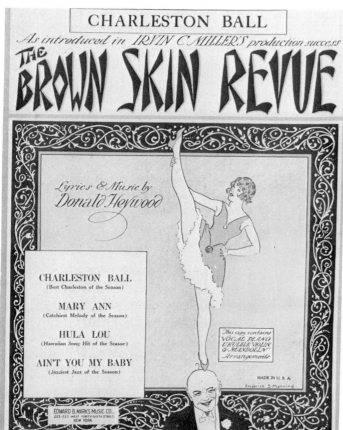

Cover for "Charleston Ball" from *The Brown Skin Revue*, 1925.

Hit of 1925, *Sunny* was first musical in which Jerome Kern teamed with Oscar Hammerstein II.

Popular song of the 1920s was used in five different productions, but eventually became known as Eddie Cantor's song. Written in 1925.

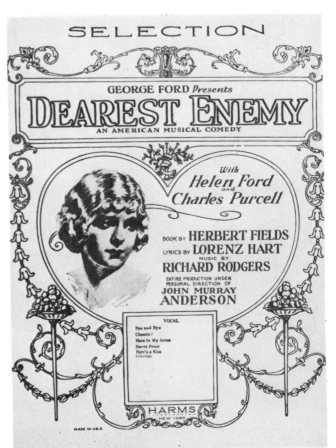

Musical of 1925 was first to be based on American history and, although written before *Garrick Gaieties*, Rodgers and Hart's first success, it was not produced until *Gaieties* had proven their talents.

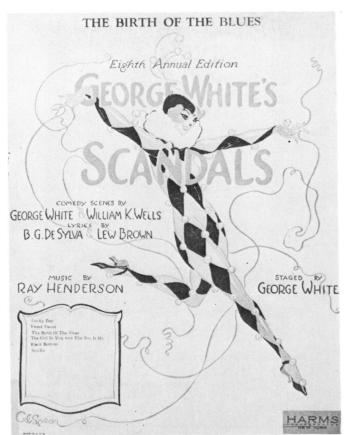

Musical revues *George White's Scandals* ran from 1919 to 1939. This well-known song from 1926 edition was introduced by Harry Richman.

Rodgers and Hart show had some of their best songs in it, and this was the biggest hit of all. Show opened in 1927.

Another 1927 hit that ran over three hundred fifty performances and was later made into film.

Oscar Hammerstein II and Jerome Kern classic, 1927.

Billed as a romantic musical comedy this operetta had one of longest runs on Broadway, 509 performances, for a Romberg musical production. It opened in 1928.

Bert Lahr gave fantastic performance in this hit of 1928.

Eddie Cantor starred again in this Ziegfeld production of 1928.

Jimmy McHugh and Dorothy Fields wrote this all-black revue which starred, for the first time on Broadway, Bill "Bojangles" Robinson. This was first hit for the writers who went on to create some of America's best-loved pop tunes.

Sweet Adeline was nostalgic show about the gay nineties. It starred Helen Morgan in 1929.

George and Ira Gershwin show of 1930 also had song, "The Man I Love."

Show of 1930 had spectacular music and lyrics and a shattering performance by Ethel Merman.

Song from eleventh edition of *George White's Scandals*, 1931.

Fred Astaire starred in this show which became *Gay Divorcee* when later made into film. Hit song from 1932 production.

Hit song from this show was "Smoke Gets in Your Eyes," 1933.

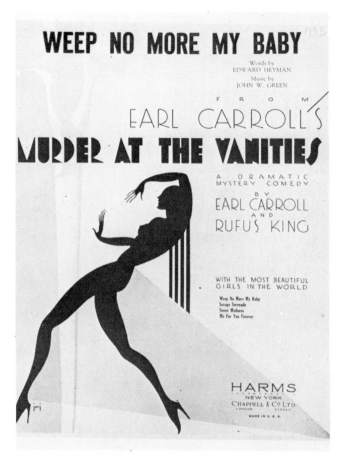

Revue that had little to recommend it except that it was later made into a movie which included the hit song "Cocktails for Two." Sheet music of 1933 also has a great Art Deco cover design by "Jorj."

Show that was Cole Porter hit of 1934.

Singer Jan Peerce introduced this standard at Radio City Music Hall in 1934.

Sophisticated cover design for Noel Coward "romantic comedy with music," 1934.

Ziegfeld died in 1932, but the *Follies* went on without him. This was prominent song from 1934 production, which also included "Wagon Wheels."

Fanny Brice was star of this *Follies* for which Vincente Minnelli did the sets. The show was Miss Brice's last appearance on Broadway.

Cover for original production of *Porgy and Bess*, George Gershwin's folk opera which opened on October 10, 1935.

Rodgers and Hart hit show of 1936. This was most popular song from show based on ballet.

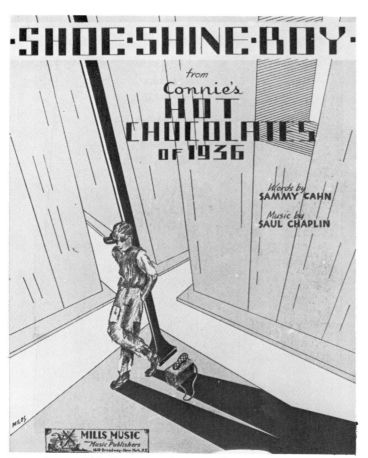

Song from all-black revue of 1936. Show with title *Hot Chocolates* was produced in 1929. This revue of 1936 was shown at Cotton Club in Harlem and was introduced by Louis Armstrong and his orchestra.

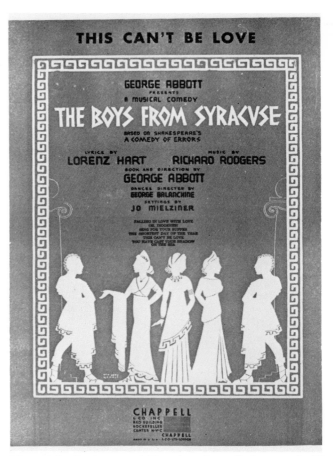

Musical by Rodgers and Hart based on Shakespeare's *The Comedy of Errors*. Show opened November 23, 1938.

Musical comedy hit of 1940 had a cast that included, among others, dancer Gene Kelly.

Gertrude Lawrence as she appeared in 1941 musical play *Lady in the Dark*.

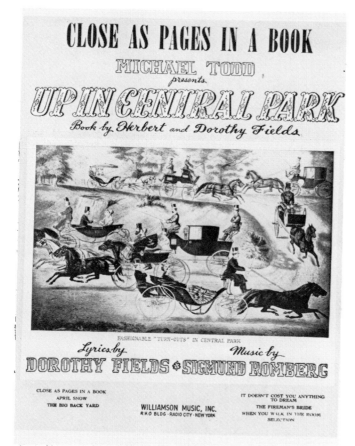

Up In Central Park had book by Herbert and Dorothy Fields, lyrics by Dorothy Fields, and music by Sigmund Romberg. Show opened in 1945.

Song from *Carousel*, hit of 1945.

Original sheet music cover from *Annie Get Your Gun*, 1946 Ethel Merman hit.

Show of 1947 with music and lyrics by Burton Lane and E. Y. Harburg.

Cole Porter show based on Shakespeare's play *The Taming of the Shrew,* opened on December 30, 1948.

Musical comedy hit of 1949 was about 1920s. Carol Channing had leading role.

Rodgers and Hammerstein's 1949 musical was outstanding work of art.

Cover for 1950 musical *Call Me Madam* has Peter Arno caricature of star, Ethel Merman.

Rodgers and Hammerstein's 1951 hit show.

Show about unions was hit in 1954.

Lerner and Loewe hit of 1956.

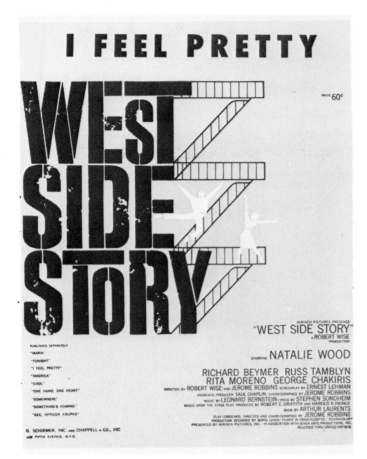

Song from *West Side Story* by Leonard Bernstein and Stephen Sondheim, 1957.

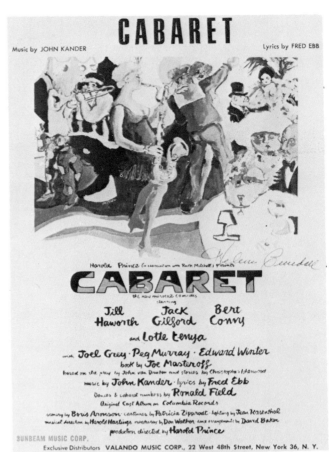

Title song from *Cabaret*, 1966 musical later made into award-winning film starring Liza Minnelli.

MOVIE MUSIC
OF THE TWENTIES,
THIRTIES, AND FORTIES

It's time to play movie music trivia. I won't make the questions too hard. What was the most extravagant setting and production in a Busby Berkeley–directed movie made in 1933? What was the first film in which Fred Astaire and Ginger Rogers danced together? Who wrote the music for the 1934 Ann Sothern film, *Let's Fall in Love*? Who directed the dances for the Warner Bros. film, *Gold Diggers of 1933*, which starred Warren William, Joan Blondell, Aline McMahon, Ruby Keeler, Dick Powell, Guy Kibbee, and Ginger Rogers? Who were the "King and Queen of the Carioca" and in what film did they do the "Continental"? From what film did the song "Alone" come? Who were the lyricist and composer for "Lovely to Look At" from the RKO picture *Roberta* of 1935? What current TV sleuth was part of the starring cast of *Broadway Melody of 1936*? Who starred in the MGM production of Cole Porter's *Rosalie*? What was Walt Disney's first full-length feature production? What movie was based on the life and music of Jerome Kern?

   Give up? The answers are all on the sheet music covers one can find for the great musical films Hollywood produced in the thirties and forties. This is only one of the reasons that movie musical sheet music is collected today. There is a wealth of historical information on the covers and this is all of interest to film buffs. In addition the photographs to be found on movie sheet music are wonderful period illustrations of how many of our best-known actors and actresses looked in their youth. By leafing through a collection of sheet music from the golden age of Hollywood musical productions one can trace the fabulous careers of such stars as Fred Astaire, Dick Powell, James Cagney, Ruby Keeler, Joan Blondell, Jack Haley, Shirley Temple, Allan Jones, Jeanette MacDonald, Nelson Eddy, Bob Hope, Bing

Crosby, June Allyson, Judy Garland, Mickey Rooney, and hundreds of others.

Long before films were made that could be advertised as "All Talking! All Singing! All Dancing!" music played an important role in the film industry. Even the smallest theater had a piano player to pound out an accompaniment to the "silents" of the twenties. The largest theaters had a "mighty Wurlitzer," or even a full orchestra, but the music added excitement as the heroine was finally untied from the railroad tracks seconds before the train arrived. The theater musician was responsible for choosing the musical themes that represented heroes and villains in the early days. Later on, the movie studios sent along suggested scores to be played with the silent films.

By the mid-twenties, when radio and records could help promote the films, theme music was written for the movies and was played live before the film came on. "Charmaine" was the theme song for *What Price Glory?* and "Ramona" was written to exploit the silent motion picture of the same title that starred Dolores Del Rio. The song was a hit before the picture was even released, and Paul Whiteman played it on his national radio program with the star of the picture doing the vocal. An especially interesting aspect of this milestone promotion was that Whiteman and Miss Del Rio were three thousand miles apart when the radio performance was given, and the technological aspects of the introduction of the song were given national publicity. When the picture was released the song was already so popular that Dolores Del Rio was sent on a personal tour from coast to coast, and she sang the song in the country's leading movie theaters. The sheet music sale totalled over two million and the various recordings sold in the several millions. All this happened before movies made a sound of their own.

As soon as the talkies came along music played an important part in their success. It is significant that the first talking picture to be produced was *The Jazz Singer,* which starred Al Jolson. The movie was first shown in October 1927, and shortly after its release the silent film had become obsolete. Soon all movies were talking and many were singing and dancing as well. Not only the entertainers but the composers and lyricists as well as much of the book material were, like Al Jolson, imported to Hollywood from New York.

The first truly significant production that can be called a real movie musical was *The Broadway Melody* of 1929. It had an original score written by Nacio Herb Brown and Arthur Freed, and the songs they wrote for the film were outstanding. The title song was a hit, as were "Wedding of the Painted Doll," and "You Were Meant for Me." The story was about show business, and it set the stage for many backstage musicals that were to follow.

The earliest musicals were all somewhat alike, and the production of them was beset with problems of a technical nature that have been best chronicled in a film made in 1952, *Singin' in the Rain.* The title song was used earlier in MGM's *Hollywood Revue,* and it was a hit first time around. The early period of movie musicals had some extravagant productions, and Universal Studios imported Paul Whiteman and his band to star in *The King of Jazz.*

One spectacular set was a huge grand piano on which the entire band was seated. There was a singing group in the picture called the Rhythm Boys, and one of the trio was a youth whose name was Bing Crosby.

The revue form of musical theater was used a lot by early Hollywood and everyone danced, sang, and was expected to adapt to comedy routines. Those who couldn't sing and dance found it increasingly difficult to get work. Gloria Swanson was certainly no accomplished singer and she mainly stuck to drama, but songs were included in some of her films and two of the best known of these were "Love, Your Spell is Everywhere" and "Come to Me." Silent actresses who didn't sing fell by the wayside. Clara Bow was one of them. Janet Gaynor was one star who made an adjustment from the silents to the musicals, and the favorite couple of the early musicals was Buddy Rogers and Nancy Carroll. Other faces that became familiar through the musicals of the early Hollywood talkies were Helen Kane (of Boo-Poo-Poo-Do fame), Jeanne Eagels, Jimmy Durante, Helen Morgan, Eddie Cantor, Ethel Waters, Fannie Brice, and Sophie Tucker. Stage stars Alexander Gray, Bernice Clair, Vivienne Seagal, Walter Pidgeon, Irene Bordoni, Jack Buchanan, Maurice Chevalier, George Jessel, and Jeanette MacDonald all went to Hollywood. Ginger Rogers and Ethel Merman made short films in New York studios before either of them was lured to the west coast.

Of all the Broadway stars who went to Hollywood Maurice Chevalier was by far the most popular in the earliest movie musical days. Among his most popular songs from films were "My Ideal," "Louise," "You Brought a New Kind of Love to Me," and "One Hour with You." Long before Jeanette MacDonald was teamed with Nelson Eddy she had a hit with Chevalier in *The Love Parade*. The two were also starred in the Rodgers and Hart musical *Love Me Tonight*.

Operettas that had been successful on stage were brought to film and Sigmund Romberg's and Rudolf Friml's music thrilled the audiences in movie theaters. Marilyn Miller danced her way through her biggest hit, *Sally*, but by this time the movie musical was beginning to lose its popularity. There would be a short respite before the films *Flying Down to Rio* and *Forty-second Street* would start an entirely new cycle in musical film.

There were hundreds of songs from the first Hollywood musicals that sold sheet music by the millions and were helped along by the recording and radio industries. Only a few can be listed here, and any selection has to be highly personal. "Tiptoe Through the Tulips" (Al Dubin, Joe Burke) from *Gold Diggers of Broadway*; "My Man" (Channing Pollock, Maurice Vain) from *My Man* and "I'm an Indian" from the same Fanny Brice show; "Am I Blue" (Grant Clarke and Harry Akst), sung by Ethel Waters in *On with the Show*; "Sonny Boy" (DeSylva, Brown, and Henderson) and "There's a Rainbow Round My Shoulder" (Billy Rose, Al Jolson, and Dave Dreyer) from *The Singing Fool*; "If I Had a Talking Picture of You" (DeSylva, Brown, and Henderson) from *Sunny Side Up*; "You Brought a New Kind of Love to Me" (Irving Kahal, Pierre Norman, Sammy Fain) from *The Big*

Pond; "Happy Days Are Here Again" (Jack Yellen, Milton Agar) from *Chasing Rainbows;* "Hooray for Captain Spalding" (Bert Kalmar, Harry Ruby) from *Animal Crackers;* "Peach of a Pair" (George Marion, Jr., Richard Whiting) from *Follow Through;* "Never Swat a Fly" (DeSylva, Brown, and Henderson) from *Just Imagine;* "Beyond the Blue Horizon" (Robin, Harling, and Whiting) from *Monte Carlo;* "My Ideal" (Robin, Whiting, Chase) from *Playboy of Paris;* "Making Whoopee" (Kahn, Donaldson) and "My Baby Just Cares For Me" from *Whoopee;* "When Your Lover Has Gone" (E. A. Swan) from *Blonde Crazy;* "Out of Nowhere" (Ed Heyman, Johnny Green) from *Dude Ranch;* "Reaching For the Moon" (Irving Berlin) from the movie of the same name; and "Love Me Tonight," "Isn't It Romantic," and "Lover" (Richard Rodgers, Lorenz Hart) from *Love Me Tonight.*

By 1932 it was time for musicals of the film world to begin making a comeback and they did—with a bang. Warner Bros., who had made the first and the best musicals and some of the earliest color musicals such as *On with the Show* and *Gold Diggers of Broadway,* had pretty much given up on musicals, but their promotion for their 1932 film, *Forty-second Street,* included a transcontinental train filled with stars and starlets (Bette Davis was included), and the film is today considered a landmark in the first revival of the film musical. If the earlier films with music had been somewhat derivative of Broadway productions of the era, *Forty-second Street* introduced a new element that became associated only with Hollywood films—the Busby Berkeley song-and-dance numbers. These were extravaganzas that could not have been produced in any other medium, and they revived American musical film.

The songs from *Forty-second Street* were written by Harry Warren and Al Dubin, and the stars were Ruby Keeler and Dick Powell, who were newcomers. Bebe Daniels, Warner Baxter, Guy Kibbee, George Brent, Una Merkel, and Ginger Rogers were also in the cast that included Girls-Girls-Girls. Besides the title song there were "Shuffle off to Buffalo," "Young and Healthy," and "You're Getting to Be a Habit With Me." The film was an enormous success and many, many more films based on the formula of *Forty-second Street* would follow in quick succession. Warners was first, but every other major studio would be close behind.

The formula was so successful that Warners followed itself immediately with another winner, *Footlight Parade,* which included James Cagney and Joan Blondell with the proven winning team of Keeler and Powell. In this picture Busby Berkeley outdid himself with "By a Waterfall," a gigantic aquacade number (Hollywood's first) in which he had hydraulic lifts to pump 20,000 gallons of water a minute over the falls and used 100 girls in the chorus. The scene was used as a background for the cover of the sheet music of "By a Waterfall," written by Irving Kahal and Sammy Fain. Obviously, with production numbers like these plot and character development were unimportant. What you remembered were the unbelievably extravagant dances and the marvelous songs from these shows. *Gold Diggers of 1933* was another big production movie with songs like "Petting in the Park" and "Shadow Waltz."

The establishment by Warners of the movie couple was also part of the formula that was followed by other producers. Ruby Keeler and Dick Powell might have been the first, but perhaps the most famous were Fred Astaire and Ginger Rogers, who were first paired in secondary roles in *Flying Down to Rio*, billed as "the aerial musical picture." Music for this picture was written by Vincent Youmans and included "Carioca," "Music Makes Me," "Orchids in the Moonlight," and the title song. The film launched the collective careers of Rogers and Astaire, each of whom has had a long and successful film life, both together and separately. Although Ginger Rogers and Fred Astaire tried other partners in between and after the movies that they made together, the pair had their most important success in films such as *Roberta, Follow the Fleet,* and *Swing Time*. They can be seen dancing their way across sheet music covers for such classic pop tunes as "Smoke Gets in Your Eyes (Otto Harbach and Jerome Kern), "Lovely to Look At" (Harbach, Kern), "But Where Are You?" (Irving Berlin), "The Way You Look Tonight" (Jerome Kern and Dorothy Fields), "They Can't Take That Away from Me" (George and Ira Gershwin), and scores of others.

The formula films were aided and abetted by more musicals from Broadway, and *Anything Goes* came to Hollywood to be produced with that new crooning sensation who started as one of the Rhythm Boys with Paul Whiteman's orchestra, Harry Lillis Crosby, better known as Bing. Crosby crooned his way through college pictures, "big broadcast" movies, and the many "road" pictures he made with Bob Hope and Dorothy Lamour. His photo is on hundreds of pieces of the best sheet music written for film. He later proved his acting ability in some successful nonmusicals, but "early Crosby" is still a popular sheet music category for collectors. Crosby's rendition of Irving Berlin's classic "White Christmas" was so popular that it was repeated in a second film named for the song. The film in which it first appeared was *Holiday Inn*.

To get back to famous musical couples of the film industry, there was no romantic couple more successful as a duo than Jeanette MacDonald and Nelson Eddy. Certainly not the most talented of all the musical stars, the couple appealed to the Depression audiences who found perfect escape in their renditions of "Ah! Sweet Mystery of Life" in *Naughty Marietta*, and songs from *Bittersweet, Rose Marie, Maytime, Sweethearts,* and *New Moon*. At times they were separated and given new mates, but they weren't as successful without each other.

Another phenomenon of the thirties musical film was the entertainment for and by children and the age group now referred to as teenagers. Where are the Shirley Temples, the Deanna Durbins, the Mickey Rooneys, and the Donald O'Connors of today? The talented child stars were made even more sensational by the thirties films and the companies that made them. The kids sang and danced their ways through many films in the thirties and early forties, and then it was all over. Only Judy Garland, whose talent was so great it couldn't be killed by overexposure of many films of varying quality, managed to make comeback after comeback until her death.

From Shirley Temple's first screen appearance in *Stand Up and Cheer*, the tot was an important Fox studio property. Her first film number, *Baby, Take a Bow*, was written while Shirley was visiting the set of the film and started to do some dance numbers while the music was being recorded. The story goes that the three-year-old hastily learned the words to a song that had been scribbled for her (presumably on the back of an old envelope) and within minutes was performing her first screen solo. It is said that Harold Lloyd, also on the set, exclaimed, "By God, here's another Jackie Coogan!" Miss Temple's success in *Stand Up and Cheer* catapulted her into fame and fortune before she had her second set of teeth.

Anyone who lived through the era when Shirley Temple danced and sang her way into the hearts of all but the most jaded and cynical Americans remembers with fondness certain musical numbers that were outstanding, among them her rendition of "Animal Crackers in My Soup" and "On the Good Ship Lollipop." Perhaps one of her best moments on the screen was her dance on the stairs with Bill Robinson in *The Little Colonel*.

If children had the films of Shirley Temple to look forward to in the thirties they were also given another treat in the first full-length films of the great Disney Studios. *Snow White and the Seven Dwarfs* was movie magic at its best and was followed by *Pinocchio, Dumbo, Bambi*, and others. All of the sheet music from the specially written songs of the great Disney films is very well worth collecting today as the whole area of "Disneyana" becomes more and more popular.

With the success of the Temple films and Disney's fantastic *Snow White*, other studios sent out searches for children who could sing and dance. Universal found its gold mine in Deanna Durbin, but the most valuable of all the young film properties were Judy Garland and Mickey Rooney. Donald O'Connor, Gloria Jean, Peggy Ryan, and Jane Powell were other juveniles who had their magic moments for the movie-going public. Of these, Donald O'Connor was perhaps the most enduring talent.

While Disney gave the young in heart *Snow White*, MGM made the greatest children's classic of all time, *The Wizard of Oz*, featuring the superb songs by E. Y. Harburg and Harold Arlen. The movie was an excellent vehicle for the talents of Judy Garland, the songs were the best, and the cast of Ray Bolger, Bert Lahr, Jack Haley, and Frank Morgan couldn't have been better. Miss Garland went on to make other great films such as *Meet Me in St. Louis, Easter Parade*, and two Andy Hardy films with Mickey Rooney. She was the best Hollywood could offer in musical talent, and she made many great songs even greater by her performances. Her adolescent musicals have been largely dimmed by her performance in *Wizard*, but there are many fans who still remember with great fondness the singing and dancing in the Garland films *Strike Up the Band, Broadway Melody of 1938*, and *Babes in Arms*.

There were, of course, many other stars in the musical movie firmament of the late thirties and forties. June Allyson was a favorite musical lead. Alice Faye and Don Ameche were paired off for many successful films, the most memorable of which was *Alexander's Ragtime Band*. Alice Faye also played opposite other male leads with great success. Other names that made it in musicals were Betty Grable, Frances Langford, Dan Dailey, Mitzi Gaynor, and Doris Day. Marilyn Monroe had little musical talent, but nobody seemed to care as she sang her unforgettable numbers in later musicals such as *Some Like It Hot, Gentlemen Prefer Blondes,* and *There's No Business like Show Business.*

The Hollywood music men of the fifties looked once again to Broadway for their material and put Betty Hutton in the lead for *Annie Get Your Gun,* Shirley Jones and Gordon MacRae for *Carousel,* and Vivien Blaine for *Guys and Dolls.* If the screen versions were less satisfactory than the stage productions there were many reasons for this, but the music was great and the films gave more exposure to some classic lyrics and tunes.

There was more to come by way of great musical films from Hollywood. The stars of previous years were still around. Some made it into the films of the late forties and early fifties and many new stars were made. A lot of superb songs were written especially for the new musicals and many earlier songs were revived by their use in popular films.

No popular medium can ignore a war and the films made as entertainment during World War II included some memorable songs. From Universal Pictures came *Follow the Boys* with a star-studded cast that included the Andrews Sisters, Dinah Shore, Louis Jordan, George Raft, Zorina, Donald O'Connor, Jeanette MacDonald, Peggy Ryan, and Sophie Tucker. The score wasn't bad, either, especially if you were around in those days and remember the popularity of "Is You Is, Or Is You Ain't (Ma' Baby)," "Shoo-Shoo Baby," and "Mad About Him, Sad Without Him, How Can I Be Glad Without Him Blues."

Hollywood Canteen included Cole Porter's "Don't Fence Me In," and in *Here Come the Waves* Bing Crosby sang "Ac-Cent-Tchu-Ate the Positive (Mister In-Between)," a song that blared from every juke box during the war and was eventually banned from the airwaves when it was discovered that it might have a hidden meaning. In general, though, the musical movies were intended to be escape rather than a reminder that there was a war on, and good wholesome entertainment was the reason they were produced.

The studio most responsible for the best musicals ever made was MGM. The studio had the most productive and talented man of all movie musicals from the mid-forties to the mid-fifties. Arthur Freed was the genius who was in charge at MGM during those years. Directors Vincente Minnelli and Stanley Donen worked for him. He hired Betty Comden and Adolph Green. He searched for the outstanding composers of the era and hired Lerner and Loewe. MGM already had the stars. There were Astaire, Garland, Sinatra, and that very talented dancer, Gene Kelly, who during this period was at his performing best.

Kelly danced with Fred Astaire in *Ziegfeld Follies* and soloed in many others, frequently choreographing his own routines. His dance with animated cartoons in *Anchors Aweigh* is considered a classic and his directorial work and dancing in *An American in Paris* is a musical high spot in American film. The title ballet was innovative and daring and certainly extremely ambitious.

There were many other magic screen moments of the period that involved Kelly's remarkable talents, but the best of all of them was *Singin' in the Rain*, the movie about the movies with book by Betty Comden and Adolph Green. The cast, with Donald O'Connor, Debbie Reynolds, and Jean Hagen, couldn't have been better chosen by Arthur Freed, and the dancing by Kelly, O'Connor, and Cyd Charisse is superior. Kelly also codirected the musical with Stanley Donen, and the songs by Nacio Herb Brown and Arthur Freed were perfect for the development of the plot and great period pieces for this spoof on the talkies. Since *Singin' in the Rain* is considered the best of all movie musicals, so much has been written about it that there is no point in discussing it further here. Fortunately, the film can be seen on television quite frequently and it never loses anything from repeated viewings.

Mostly, however, the golden age of film musicals starred one talent, Judy Garland, who was now grown up and appeared in many films after her fantastic performance in *The Wizard of Oz*. All through a very delayed adolescence she teamed with Mickey Rooney in two Andy Hardy pictures (at the time it seemed as though there were more), *Thoroughbreds Don't Cry*, and the musicals *Babes in Arms*, *Strike Up the Band*, *Babes on Broadway*, and the film that is the Garland-Rooney favorite of most moviegoers of the pre-1945 period, *Girl Crazy*. Judy Garland's portrayal of Esther Smith in *Meet Me in St. Louis* (1944) is considered one of the outstanding performances of her career. The film was directed by Vincente Minnelli and the following year the two were married. A great contemporary musical talent, Liza Minnelli, is the result of that union.

The songs of many of the Garland films of the forties were the hits of the period. Great Gershwin tunes were sung in *Girl Crazy*. A few were "Embraceable You," "Bidin' My Time," and "But Not for Me." The Johnny Mercer and Harry Warren song from MGM's *The Harvey Girls*, made in 1946, that won that year's Oscar was "On the Atchison, Topeka, and the Santa Fe," a perfect song for the Garland talents. In 1946 she sang two classics by Jerome Kern, "Look For the Silver Lining" and "Who?" Perhaps the highest point in Judy Garland's adult career was her performance in *A Star Is Born* in 1954.

By the fifties the films had television as a tough competitor and the heyday of the great movie musical was almost over. Two safe types of musicals were made after 1954, the biographical pictures and the film versions of shows that had already been successful on Broadway. The biopix, which gave the studios a chance to use old and previously successful music, was especially successful in the fifties. Female singers of an earlier time were portrayed on the screen and life stories were written about the bandleaders of the big band era.

The film adaptations of Broadway hits such as *Carousel, Oklahoma, South Pacific,* and *The King and I* were produced. The sheet music from these films is of little interest to collectors who would prefer finding the published music from the original shows rather than the films. Film historians have a different interest in the music that represents the musical movies of the fifties. Photographs and information are all there on the covers, and even though the great tunes of Rodgers and Hart and others can be found in earlier published editions, movie buffs prefer to own the sheet music published when the films were released. For instance, sheet music from the film *Words and Music*, based on the lives and work of Rodgers and Hart, tells us on the covers that every star under MGM contract was trotted out. We find photos of seven of the top stars, all pertinent information as to who directed the film, who produced it, who did the screenplay, and other material important to cinema historians.

One reason for the increasing interest in musical film sheet music is the tendency for filmmakers to review their industry's accomplishments periodically. They seem always to want to know where they've been, and a recent history of the MGM musicals, *That's Entertainment*, has brought attention to the fact that the films and stars of the one studio were outstanding. We can go to see the film as often as we like (when it's available), but there are few tangible souvenirs of the great movie musical period except for the sheet music and the recordings. If movie memorabilia is of any value at all, certainly the sheet music with photographic covers of wonderful action shots of singers and dancers will be among the best memorabilia we have.

Song inspired by film *Ramona* became great hit in 1927.

Theme song from 1926 film *What Price Glory?*

Gloria Swanson sang this song in 1929 film *The Trespasser.*

Cover from "Tip Toe Through the Tulips with Me" introduced in 1929 musical made by Warner.

Song from science-fiction musical of 1930 by Fox.

Ziegfeld star Ed Wynn appeared in this 1930 Paramount film, which also included Ginger Rogers.

Early dancing team is featured in 1930 film by Warner.

Winning team of Dick Powell and Ruby Keeler appeared in 1933 film. Ginger Rogers was in this one, too.

Ginger Rogers again in 1933 Paramount musical *Sitting Pretty*.

Ann Sothern is featured in glamorous pose on title song from 1934 Columbia production.

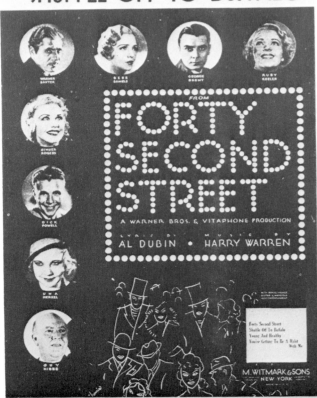

Ruby Keeler and Dick Powell landmark film of 1933.

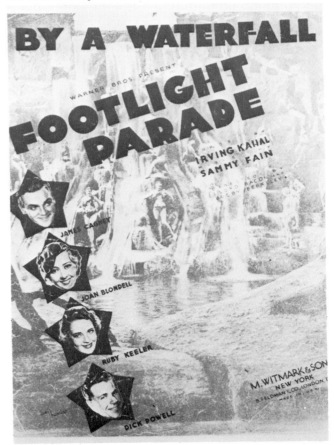

Sheet music cover from this 1933 classic film has scene of Busby Berkeley spectacular, "By a Waterfall."

Film that introduced dancing team of Astaire and Rogers shown in their big number, 1933.

Mae West in one of her most famous pictures. She starred with Cary Grant in 1933.

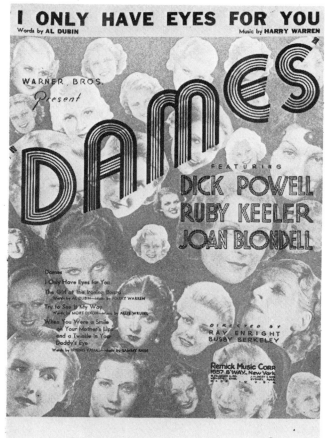

Hollywood brought many hit Broadway shows to film, this one in 1934.

Hit musical by Warner Bros. in 1934.

Ginger Rogers and Dick Powell in 1934 Warner Bros. picture.

The Marx Brothers with Allan Jones and Kitty Carlisle in one of their classic films, 1935.

Dick Powell in 1935 Warner Bros. musical.

Broadway hit was made into film in 1935 by RKO.

Star-studded cast of *Broadway Melody of 1936* included young Buddy Ebsen.

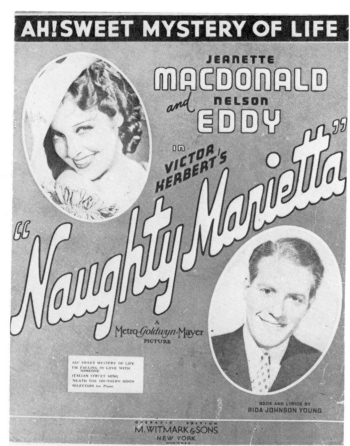

The operetta form returned with this winning couple. *Naughty Marietta*, first performed on the stage in 1910, made a comeback in 1935 film.

Shirley Temple in one of her best films, produced in 1935, danced with Bill Robinson.

Fox studio's biggest asset in 1936 film *Stowaway*.

Jean Harlow in song that was dedicated to her, 1936.

Fred Astaire and Ginger Rogers in film that featured music and lyrics by Irving Berlin, 1936.

"The Way You Look Tonight," from *Swing Time,* with music by Jerome Kern and lyrics by Dorothy Fields starred Astaire and Rogers in 1936.

Rogers and Astaire are sitting down for a change on cover of song from *Shall We Dance,* 1937.

Betty Grable film of 1937 used song written in 1910.

Song from *Gold Diggers of 1937*.

Grace Moore as she appeared in 1937 Columbia film.

Jeanette MacDonald teamed with Allan Jones in this 1912 operetta revived by MGM in 1937.

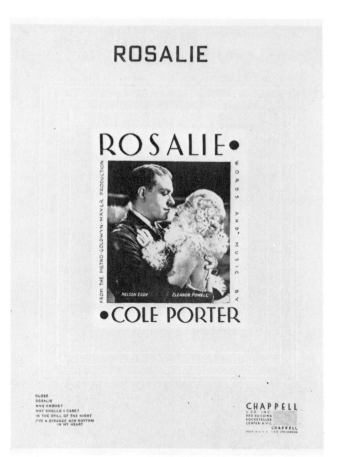

Atypical cover was designed for Cole Porter movie musical of 1937.

Song from 1938 film became theme song for Bob Hope, who had minor role in this movie.

1937 film featured score by Jerome Kern and Oscar Hammerstein and starred Irene Dunne.

Song from Walt Disney's first full-length feature film, 1937.

Goldwyn Follies, 1938, had an all-star cast that included Edgar Bergen and Charlie McCarthy. Music was by George and Ira Gershwin.

Johnny Mercer standard from Dick Powell-Olivia DeHavilland film of 1938.

One of many college musicals, this one made in 1938. It had a score by Frank Loesser and Manning Sherwin.

Biographical picture of life of Jerome Kern, 1939.

Song from film starring Charles Boyer and Irene Dunne, 1939.

Bing Crosby hit from film *The Star Maker*, 1939.

Classic film that launched Judy Garland on a fantastic and tragic career, 1939.

Disney film of 1940.

Judy Garland made two "Andy Hardy" films with Mickey Rooney. They starred together in many other pictures. Song was written in 1921 but used again in this 1940 movie.

Intermezzo was 1940 film that introduced Ingrid Bergman to American audience.

Hit song from 1941 ice extravaganza that starred Sonja Henie.

Irving Berlin's all-time Christmas hit was introduced in this film in 1942.

Rita Hayworth paired with Fred Astaire for this 1942 film.

The big bands came to Hollywood. This 1942 film featured Glenn Miller and his band.

Harry James and his Music Makers in 1942 film.

Classic song from classic film, 1942. Song was written and first published in 1931.

Period musical starring Rita Hayworth and Victor Mature was made in 1942. Songs were from turn of the century.

Hit song of 1942 was used in picture starring, among others, the Ritz Brothers.

Film made by Columbia in 1942 had score by Cole Porter and starred Don Ameche, Janet Blair, and Jack Oakie.

Wartime film had hit song from 1928 interpolated into it. Spencer Tracy and Irene Dunne in 1943.

During the big band era Benny Goodman made this film for Fox. The year was 1943.

This song was written for Bette Davis for 1943 film. It's about the wartime draft and the lack of available men.

First film that showed black performers and characters in sympathetic roles was made in 1943.

Andrews Sisters, already successful recording and radio trio, made films in 1940s. This was hit song from 1943 film *Three Cheers For the Boys.*

Fox period piece, made in 1943.

Hit song from 1943 musical starring Bing Crosby and Dorothy Lamour.

Eleanor Powell was talented dancer who starred in MGM musical in 1943.

Talented Lena Horne was always shoved into segments of films that could be removed for showing in the South. Film is 1943, song, 1929. Music was written by Fats Waller.

Hit song featured in film *Follow the Boys* was introduced by Dinah Shore in 1944.

Deanna Durbin played grown-up role in wartime film, 1943.

Rita Hayworth and Gene Kelly musical with score by Jerome Kern and Ira Gershwin, 1944.

Hit written by Cole Porter in *Hollywood Canteen*, 1944.

Movie song by Harold Arlen and Johnny Mercer was hit of 1944 film.

Betty Hutton was blonde bombshell of 1944 Paramount film.

Film of 1945 based on life of George Gershwin.

One of many "road" pictures with Bing Crosby, Bob Hope, and Dorothy Lamour, this one from 1945.

Dick Haymes starred in this Rodgers and Hammerstein musical in 1945.

Hit song performed by Judy Garland in 1945 MGM film.

Hoagy Carmichael and Jack Brooks wrote this standard for 1946 film.

College musical to end all college musicals, a DeSylva, Brown, and Henderson hit of 1947.

Biographical picture based on the lives and work of Richard Rodgers and Lorenz Hart, 1948.

Fred Astaire with dancer Vera-Ellen in MGM 1950 film.

Movie spectacular of 1952 featured music by Jerome Kern. By this time the golden age of movie musicals was over.

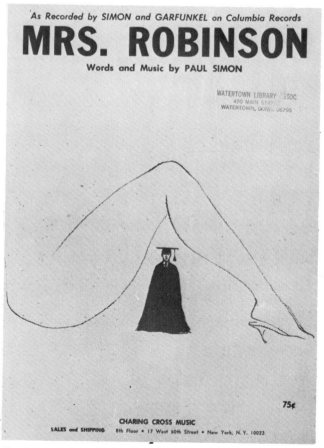

Sheet music from "Mrs. Robinson," written for 1968 film *The Graduate*.

WHATEVER HAPPENED TO THE SHEET MUSIC BUSINESS?

Although most of us have taken the publication of our popular songs in sheet music form for granted it might come as a surprise to many that you can't buy sheet music easily any more. The major happening that changed the entire music publishing business was the development of a kind of music that depended more on the performance than it did on the written score. When rock and roll became popular back in the mid-fifties the sheet music business was already diminishing. Records and radio had taken the place of the parlor piano, folk music was more easily played on a guitar, and even if you had the sheet music to a song made popular by Bill Haley and Haley's Comets it didn't sound the same when played at home. It was easier just to put on a record and turn the volume as loud as possible.

Most of the important New York music publishers had given up the business during the period when musical movies were being made, and several large publishers sold out to the studios. Others have struggled along on their backlists and some compilations of music in book form. Basically, however, the pop music business has changed so drastically in the past twenty-five years that the Tin Pan Alley promoters would never recognize it. The men who went out and plugged their company's songs in the first two decades of this century probably would find it difficult to believe that it just doesn't pay to sell sheet music any longer.

In the old days songs were plugged in a number of ways. A salesman would go from night clubs to vaudeville theaters to try to talk the most popular performers into interpolating a new song into an existing act. A favorite way of plugging a new song during the old vaudeville days was to plant a singer in the audience and have him sing the song from there as if spontaneously deciding that it was the proper moment to burst into song. The younger the singer, and many young boys with soprano voices were used, the more possibility that the song would be a hit. Wagons were loaded up with instruments and musicians who played new songs in the streets.

In the days of early radio that medium was used to plug songs, and we have already seen that the broadcasters thought that was all the payment the music publishers should get for the use of their music. In the days before ASCAP all music could be played in any public place without payment. The total income to the composers and the publishers was what they could derive from the sale of the physical sheet music.

The recording industry, especially since the invention of the long-playing record, has changed all that. This didn't happen overnight, however, and for many years before rock, sheet music sales continued, although at a rate much reduced from the earlier part of this century. The record companies made the most money from any new song, but the music publisher had some sales. Moreover, the records were all made by a few major companies, and the music was also published by a few publishers who still survived.

Along with the popularity of folk music and rock there developed many independent recording companies, mostly owned by successful performers. Many also published their own songs. It is interesting to read the publishers of the sheet music for rock songs that can be found. Elvis Presley formed his own publishing company and "Love Me Tender" has the imprint Elvis Presley Music, Inc. While the early Beatles song, "I Want to Hold Your Hand," was published by a subsidiary of Music Corporation of America, slightly later songs such as "Hello, Goodbye" and "Penny Lane" were published by the Beatle-owned company, Maclen Music, Inc.

Collectors seem to sense when the time is right to begin to preserve American artifacts relating to an important aspect of American history that has become a closed chapter. This is obviously true of American popular sheet music. Except through the published music sheets there is no other way to preserve the entire story of popular music and musical theater and film history. At first sheet music was collected for its value as art and, second, for what it tells us of the musical history of the past two centuries. Now it is collected because there is no better way to get the information about musical history in America than to study the covers of the published songs.

Age is not an especially important criterion any longer for collectible sheet music. Any popular song that is significant in some way to American musical history, whether old or recent, is worth saving. Certainly, the music of the individuals and groups who contributed to the greatest phenomena of musical change in this century is important to document now. There was so little of it available that Presley, the Beatles, Sly and the Family Stone, the Doors, and other groups' rock and roll should be preserved. It's not that these performers are ready for the grave, but that their appearances have changed as rapidly as the style of music for which they have been responsible. Where it used to take twenty or thirty years for a standard to become a "Golden Oldie," in the world of rock this happens almost overnight. Yesterday's hit is today's collectible. There is already a cult of "Beatlemania" among the generation who grew up knowing nothing but rock and roll. This is a generation that knows it was so fickle when it came to the popular music of its era that it was "Hello, Goodbye" in very fast order.

Charles Calhoun on one of earliest rock and roll hits, "Shake, Rattle, and Roll," 1954.

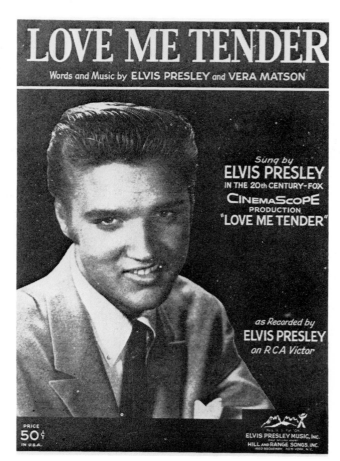

Elvis Presley on cover of music to "Love Me Tender," 1956.

The Beatles on the cover of their 1963 hit.

The Beatles again in more artistic cover for hit from 1967.

"Penny Lane," Beatles song from 1967.

"Get Back," hit of 1969, has writers John Lennon and Paul McCartney on front cover and all four Beatles on back cover.

Cover for 1968 number recorded by Sly and the Family Stone.

The Doors, silhouetted in black against a white background on cover for 1968 song.

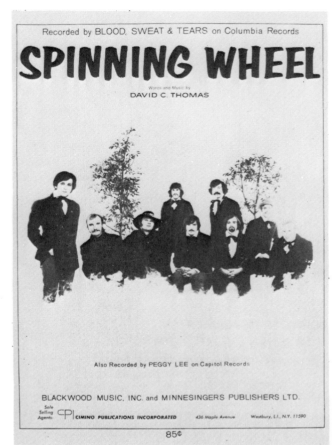

The rock group, Blood, Sweat and Tears, looks as though it were photographed in the nineteenth century on the 1968 cover for "Spinning Wheel."

SPECIALIZED COLLECTING

There is no area that has such a wealth of material still available as the collecting of America's songs and musical pieces. The field is so vast and varied that only a few of the many collectible categories can be discussed in one book, and only a small portion of the outstanding examples of worthwhile covers can be illustrated. Of the roughly two and a half million songs and musical pieces that have been written and published in this country, a great percentage of these have covers that are illustrated. Many have artistic significance. However, few serious studies have been done to sort out two hundred years of musical paper ephemera. The main reason for this is that attention has been given mainly to what is between the covers. Sheet music has historically been more often heard than seen.

There have been few museum exhibits of sheet music covers and this is probably due to the fact that the great music collections in this country repose where they properly belong—in the music departments of libraries and universities. The covers are seldom seen by art historians who would be more concerned with the visual rather than the melodic aspects of sheet music. Print collections in art museums do not often include many, if any, of the early lithographs to be found in abundance on sheet music covers of the first half of the nineteenth century. Music library collections are not often put on public display unless they happen to tie in with some other artifacts. For instance, Lafayette covers may be seen from time to time, but they are usually displayed with other souvenirs of 1824–25. Political covers are sometimes given attention during an election year. The covers that have handsome hand-colored lithographs of sailing ships and whalers of the nineteenth century are sometimes included in displays of nautical material, and minstrel music is just beginning to be taken out of the closet.

Throughout the history of printed sheet music in America some of our most capable artists have earned a living designing covers that are clever and original. It is little known in the art world, for instance, that Winslow Homer, the great American painter, worked for the lithographer Bufford between the years 1855 and 1857. He illustrated sheet music covers in that time. An early Homer design, signed with his initials, is the illustration on the cover of "The Wheelbarrow Polka." The cover shows Major Benjamin Perley Poore pushing a wheelbarrow full of apples from Newbury to Boston after having lost an election bet with Colonel Robert I. Burbank. When Poore reached his destination, a distance of some thirty-six miles, there were thirty thousand onlookers to greet him.

Historians of the development of the art and science of photography would have a strong interest in sheet music covers if they were aware that all new developments in photography were used to illustrate them. The cover of "Lady! The Rose I Give to Thee" would be as unimportant as the music within were it not decorated with a photograph of Lady Shaw to whom the piece was dedicated. The picture is an early example of a photographic technique called Plumbeotype. This was a method of transferring daguerreotype pictures to paper for lithographing purposes. So little of this work was done that the 1845 sheet music cover is a rare example.

Autographed sheet music covers are another category of collecting that deserves mention. A number of examples of these can be found. Value, of course, depends upon the connection of the autographer to the cover. A copy of the "Pickwick Polka" written in honor of Charles Dickens's visit to the United States in 1867 and signed by him is an important item. Another type of autographed cover is one that has been signed by the lyricist or composer or the performer who introduced the song.

Other types of covers for which the collector might search are songs written in honor of the innovations and inventions of the nineteenth century. Some of these have already been discussed. There were songs written in honor of the telephone such as Charles K. Harris' "Hello, Central (Give Me Heaven)" and at least one composer paid homage to Edison's new invention, the phonograph.

Sheet music cover designers and printers have probably never thought of their work as anything more than an inexpensive form of decoration that hopefully would attract the eye of a buyer long enough to convince him to take the song off the rack. Only a few artists ever signed their work. There have been a few covers made, not usually for very memorable songs, that had separately printed pictures pasted to the music cover. "Helen's Babies in Their Little Bed" is only worth collecting because it does have an applied color print on the cover.

For those who are interested in the development of popular art styles through two centuries there is no better place to study them than on a comprehensive collection of the songs that have been popular through our history. The turn-of-the-century border design on Harris's "Always in the Way" and the handsome picture of that old favorite "Red Wing" could not have been designed at any other time in our art history. The cover of a song of adultery (a subject unusual in itself in 1911) titled "If You Talk in Your Sleep Don't Mention My Name," is an excellent example of the transitional art style that bridged Art Nouveau and Art Deco.

The cover for the song "Jealous" is interesting because it is one of the relatively few illustrations done by a well-known artist of the period. Frederick Manning was rightly proud of his paintings of fashionable young women, and the 1924 cover is typical of the poster and magazine illustrations being done in the twenties. Late twenties and thirties song hits were often decorated with the cubistic and stylized designs that came into vogue and that seemed to appeal to the commerical artists of the period. A particularly original example of this new art is the cover for "Gloomy Sunday," one of the bluest of blues songs ever written.

Novelty sheet music covers have great appeal for many collectors. For example, a song that made no hit parades and would never have been heard from since its original issue is of interest only to collectors of novelty covers. The cover design aptly fits the subject and title of the song. The illustration of bandleader Freddy Martin on the cover of "Somebody Goofed" is intentionally placed upside down and thereby is illustrative of the song's subject.

The publication of sheet music used to be an enormous and lucrative industry, and the hiring of talented artists for cover design and layout was a worthwhile investment. With the increasing popularity of rock and roll in the sixties and seventies the record business skyrocketed. Although the record industry and the published song business have always been interdependent, there is less and less call for the sheet music of new songs. Hardly anybody stands around the piano and sings any more and if they do, they have found that for that purpose the old songs are the best songs. What used to be a major form of active entertainment has given way to the more passive forms of listening to music on stereo or watching television. There is little good art to be found on the sheet music covers that are published today. All of the music industry's artistic effort and expenditure go into the design of the more lucrative record album covers. The best of these, too, will one day be considered excellent examples of popular art and they will be the collectors' items of the future.

Lithograph for this cover was made by Winslow Homer in 1856.

Portrait done by Plumbeotype process in 1845.

Autographed cover of "Pickwick Polka," 1868.

Cover with pasted-on picture in color is unusual and collectible.

Music written in honor of newspaper, 1893.

Sheet music that was inserted as a supplement to newspapers. This was printed on very cheap paper and few have survived.

Music sheet given away to advertise medicine is in demand by bottle collectors today.

Sheet music that was given away to promote the sale of "Fish Bitters" in 1868.

Advertising music to promote the image of sewing machine company in 1891.

"Regina March" helped promote the sale of music boxes in 1895.

CARE AND REPAIR OF OLD SHEET MUSIC

There are only a few types of damages to which old lithographed prints are prone. These damages are usually more often found on sheet music than any other type of print, since many pieces of sheet music once had a lot of handling and when new were never treated as works of art. The most common problem one finds is that the prints have soiled borders. If this is only surface dirt it can be removed by rubbing gently with an art gum eraser. Be very careful to remove only the dirt and not the surface of the paper.

Small tears along the edge of the old sheet music covers can be repaired at home. If the tears are old they might require some cleaning before they are fixed. Open the music and lay the torn edges on a clean flat surface. Use a soft-bristled brush soaked in clear warm water (an old soft toothbrush will do), and lifting one edge gently with a pair of tweezers, carefully brush the other towards the tear. Do the same thing with the other side. This will eliminate a dirty line that might show once the tear has been pasted. The entire print can then be placed in a large plastic pan such as those used for washing photographic prints and clear warm water run into the pan for five or ten minutes. The print can then be removed and blotted. The damp print is then placed between two pieces of blotting paper and clamped together, sandwich-fashion, between two pieces of plywood and left until thoroughly dry. This may take several days.

Once the print is clean and dry, the tear may be repaired by cutting a piece of rice paper to fit over the tear. Use only as much paper as necessary. Wheat paste is best for repairing torn paper since it will not pucker. If the tear is a small one brush paste on the edges of the tear, and using a clean dry brush, work the feathered edges together. The rice paper can then be glued onto the back to reinforce the repair.

Never attempt to wash a print that has any handpainting on it. This can be done by a professional print restorer, and since the colored lithographs are the most valuable pieces of old sheet music, it is well worth the investment to have them restored by an expert. The same is true of paper that has small brown spots in it. These spots, called foxing, are caused by the growth of a fungus in the paper and require special attention to keep them from spreading.

All of the above directions and advice apply only to the early lithographed sheet music that was printed on heavy paper. Later sheet music was printed on a cheaper quality of coated paper, and little can be done to restore damages short of repairing tears with tape and erasing surface dirt. Even erasures are a problem on this later paper, since any injudicious rubbing can remove print and color. Later sheet music is generally inexpensive, and the collector should only add to his collection examples that are in relatively good condition. When a piece of later sheet music does have a tear it can be repaired with clear pre-glued tape of the type used by libraries for book repair. The tape should be applied to the inside of the cover. Do not attempt to wash or clean the later paper with any sort of liquid, not even water. The paper will simply disintegrate. Keep all paste and glue away from later sheet music also. It will wrinkle the paper.

Music libraries that own large collections of early sheet music have boxes made specially of rag board for safe storage. The boxes have one side that opens easily so that the music sheets can be slid out with as little stress as possible to the paper. The box openings overlap when closed to keep out dust and air. Collectors can use clear plastic food storage bags for storing their most treasured examples of sheet music. Bags of one gallon capacity with fold-lock tops are best and will fit most sheet music. This type of protection is advantageous because it prevents the music sheets from sticking to one another. The sheets can be handled with no further soiling and each piece can easily be seen and identified.

Many collectors like to frame their most colorful examples of sheet music to use as wall decoration. If this is to be done with any early sheet music of value there are several rules to follow. The first seems almost too obvious to mention, but many early pieces of sheet music have been ruined simply because the music itself was not considered to be as important as the cover illustration. Do *not* cut the cover from the rest of the music. Also, do not cut the borders of the cover to fit an existing frame.

An airtight unit should be made by first taping together on all four sides the glass, mat, print, and backboard before they are put into the frame. This will prevent the disintegration of the print by the entry of dirt and dampness. Both the mat and backboard should be made of rag-content board. Wood fibre cardboard should never come in contact with an old print since this hastens the growth of brown spots.

The airtight unit should then be placed in a frame and a piece of brown paper cut to fit the back. This paper is then glued to the frame. The backing paper should be checked every few years and, if necessary, replaced. Framed in this manner the early examples of hand-painted lithographed sheet music can be handsome room decorations. Their value will not decrease if they are hung out of strong sunlight and given a reasonable amount of attention.

All sheet music, whether old or new, should be stored flat and never should be rolled. This is especially true of any old lithographed music covers since rolling is extremely damaging to a print. If music has been rolled it should be placed face down on a clean surface and flattened by putting some heavy weights on it for whatever period of time it takes for the piece to lie flat by itself.

As more and more collectors join the ranks of those who are interested in owning and preserving examples of the early lithographed prints on American sheet music, supplies will become even more scarce than they are. Early sheet music should be kept in as good condition as possible. If you have pieces with small tears or that show evidence of foxing and you are not willing to become knowledgeable in the restoration of old prints, do not hesitate to spend the money to have the music repaired by an expert. Only you can tell whether a particular piece of sheet music is worth the investment of proper preservation. The print expert may tell you that the print is not of great importance, but he is not usually that knowledgeable about the historical value of a piece of old music.

ABOUT COLLECTING SHEET MUSIC AS A HOBBY

A lot has been written about popular American music of the past two centuries. Encyclopedic works that list composers, lyricists, and titles abound in our libraries. The development of music as a popular art form has been analyzed by many specialists in the field, and the lyrics of popular American songs have been discussed at length in many books, some of a serious nature and others, especially those written by Sigmund Spaeth, in a humorous vein. Very little attention has been given to the visual aspects of published American sheet music. Another neglected area of study is the historical value of published sheet music.

In 1916 O. G. Sonneck, then chief of the Music Division of the Library of Congress, in speaking before members of the Music Teachers National Association, said, "The interests of a historian of music and musical life are not, and ought not to remain, confined to matters of musical aesthetics or technique. If we can but seldom take pride in such music as music, then at least let us rejoice in the fact that quite often its pictorial title pages—a fashion probably imported from France—give us aesthetic satisfaction or afford instructive glimpses into olden times." Mr. Sonneck spoke before the greatest of American popular songs had even been written. The American musical theater was still in the future. If he had been addressing art historians rather than musicologists and musicians some interest might have arisen in the wealth of historical prints to be found on sheet music covers of the previous century. As it was, little attention was paid at the time to sheet music as an example of American popular art history.

The first article to appear that concerned the artistic aspect of sheet music covers was published in the magazine *Antiques* in November 1927. It was in the twenties that there was a renewed interest in collecting and preserving the prints of Currier and Ives, and several writers mentioned the early sheet music covers lithographed by Nathaniel Currier before his partnership with

Ives. However, only one writer, Jane Cooper Bland, listed some fifty covers done by Currier in her book, *Currier and Ives, A Manual for Collectors.*

In 1933 a two-part article written by Edith A. Wright and Josephine A. McDevitt was published in *Antiques,* stressing the importance of the early sheet music covers from an artistic and historic point of view. The article listed some of the American lithographers who made covers for sheet music before 1870. Doubtless, by this time there were already some collectors who had become fascinated by what was then a relatively inexpensive hobby. Supplies of early sheet music at the time must have been rather ample and certainly the prices were low.

The most important work on the subject of collectible sheet music covers was written in 1941 by two collectors from Philadelphia, Harry Dichter and Elliott Shapiro. The book covers many of the most important songs written before 1889, and it includes a valuable list of song publishers and lithographers of the nineteenth century. Unfortunately, there are only thirty-two photographs of the illustrated covers, but the information given in the book is an invaluable source for the many collectors that *Early American Sheet Music, Its Lure and Its Lore* inspired. In 1947 Mr. Dichter, who became a dealer in old sheet music as well as a collector, published an illustrated catalogue of music that he had available for sale with prices. This book is now a collector's item itself, as are the two subsequent Dichter catalogues.

Many of the great collections of sheet music in our libraries and universities either were started or were augmented by the collections begun privately in the thirties and forties. As often happens, it is the private collectors who are the first to see the historical and artistic importance of many forms of popular art. Meanwhile, collecting American sheet music as a hobby has grown nationally, and competition for available early lithographed sheet music is strong. Collectors now have a national organization to which they can belong, and members contribute information to the club's publication. The National Sheet Music Society, Inc., P. O. Box 2235, Pasadena, California 91105, is a necessary aid to the spread of an enjoyable and rewarding hobby.

If the collecting and preservation of our nation's popular music was slow to get started, it now has thousands of devotees who become more knowledgeable all the time about which songs might be of historical or artistic importance in the future. A study of the people and events that inspired songs in the past gives some insight into what will be important in the future. Fortunately, there are many collectors who are able to look beyond the snobbery of age when it comes to preserving our musical heritage. Songs of this century are now being carefully put away, and many are already in short supply and great demand. Sheet music is a part of the nation's paper ephemera that was used and not especially saved when it had gone out of style. For those pieces of music that were saved, we may be grateful to some knowledgeable musicologists, some housekeepers who never throw anything away, and mainly, the collectors who knew what they were preserving.

INDEX